Reginald Blunt

The Carlyles' Chelsea Home

Reginald Blunt

The Carlyles' Chelsea Home

ISBN/EAN: 9783744714334

Printed in Europe, USA, Canada, Australia, Japan

Cover: Foto ©ninafisch / pixelio.de

More available books at **www.hansebooks.com**

The

Carlyles' Chelsea Home,

being some account of

No. 5, Cheyne Row,

BY

REGINALD BLUNT.

"Could each here vow to do his little task even as the Departed did his great one: in the manner of a true man, not for a Day, but for Eternity! To live, as he counselled and commanded, not commodiously in the Reputable, the Plausible, the Half, but resolutely in the Whole, the Good, the True:

"Im Ganzen, Guten, Wahren resolut zu leben!"
CARLYLE (*Death of Goethe*).

LONDON : GEORGE BELL AND SONS,
YORK STREET, COVENT GARDEN.
1895.

"TOWARDS·ENGLAND
NO·MAN·HAS·BEEN,·&
DONE,·LIKE·YOU."

From Sterling's last letter to Carlyle

PREFATORY NOTE.

THE following pages contain no biography of Carlyle. Had I cherished any such rash intention, the fifty-six closely printed columns of the "Bibliography" at the end of Dr. Garnett's "Life of Carlyle" would surely have been sufficient to extinguish it. A couple of thousand —at a rough guess—of lives, memoirs, studies, reminiscences, essays, and articles upon Carlyle and all his works, seems, for the moment, enough, and more than enough. "The cloud of witnesses, good, bad, and indifferent," is in danger of obscuring the rugged outline about which they have gathered so thickly. I have only aimed at a much more modest enterprise.

Those who are interested in Carlyle's House are presumably conversant with the main features of what was, in the common acceptance of the term, an uneventful life.

All that is attempted here is to give some authentic record of the home existence in the unpretentious dwelling which sheltered Thomas Carlyle and his wife from 1834 till their deaths, and to give it, as far as possible, in their own words, illustrated by the contemporary records of their friends.

b

As regards both text and illustrations, I have gratefully to acknowledge the most kindly assistance from several sources.

Messrs. Longmans, Green, and Co. have given permission for the use of the various extracts from the "History of Carlyle's Life in London" and the "Reminiscences by Thomas Carlyle."

Mr. Robert Tait, who was an intimate friend at "No. 5" in and after the fifties, and who was fortunately a skilful amateur photographer as well as an artist, in days when the former pursuit was much more arduous than now, has been so good as to place at my disposal a number of excellent and valuable ñegatives, from which the portraits of Mr. and Mrs. Carlyle have been reproduced by photogravure, and the views of the garden and the garret room by the zincographic process.

Mrs. Allingham, who was a frequent visitor at Cheyne Row in later years, and who made there a number of valuable sketches and drawings, has also given valuable help; and I am indebted to Mr. Charles Baly for the loan of some negatives taken by him in the dining and drawing-rooms of the house in 1881.

Neighbourhood is a very modest qualification; but its stimulus must be my apology for this small undertaking. Most of my life has been spent within stone-throw of Cheyne Row. It was at this garden gate that Carlyle looked for the last time on Edward Irving, as he turned the corner, after his one visit to their Chelsea home; and dim, boyish memories recall the comings of Mr. and Mrs. Carlyle; the long pipes and long talks at the old Rectory, whose stable housed the noble Fritz; whose cows (their pasturage is now Bramerton Street!) supplied the morning milk which Mrs. Carlyle so much appreciated; and whose mulberries, from the venerable Elizabethan tree in its garden, it was my privilege, in their season, to carry to "No. 5."

It was from this Rectory, too, in 1881, that the movement was originated which placed Boehm's beautiful statue of Carlyle in the Embankment Garden. Latterly the wretched condition of the house in Cheyne Row made constant appeal to us who passed its neglected threshold almost daily; and it is therefore the greater pleasure to have been associated with the effort which has resulted in its timely preservation.

R. B.

Chelsea Rectory,

September, 1895

Biography of Teufelsdröckh there is, clearly enough, none to be gleaned here: at most some sketchy, shadowy fugitive likeness of him.

THE MOTTO TO

"SARTOR RESARTUS,"

THE LIFE AND OPINIONS OF HERR TEUFELSDRÖCKH.

Mein Vermächtniß, wie herrlich weit und breit!
Die Zeit ist mein Vermächtniß, mein Acker ist die Zeit.

RENDERED BY CARLYLE

(*Slightly reduced facsimile*)

*These lines were old favourites of Carlyle's, often quoted by him.
The above translation was written for my father in 1867. At the
end of the Essay " Characteristics " (1831) they are thus given:*

"My inheritance, how wide and fair !
Time is my fair seed-field, of Time I'm heir."

> A Great Soul, living apart; endeavouring to speak-forth the inspiration that was in him by Printed Books.

CONTENTS.

> If now we ask what our degree of progress, during these Ten Chapters, has been, towards right understanding, let not our discouragement become total.

> 𝔚𝔥𝔞𝔱 𝔦𝔣 𝔥𝔢𝔯𝔢 𝔴𝔢 𝔥𝔞𝔡 𝔫𝔬 𝔡𝔦𝔯𝔢𝔠𝔱 𝕮𝔞𝔪𝔢𝔯𝔞-
> 𝔬𝔟𝔰𝔠𝔲𝔯𝔞 𝔓𝔦𝔠𝔱𝔲𝔯𝔢 𝔬𝔣 𝔱𝔥𝔢 𝔓𝔯𝔬𝔣𝔢𝔰𝔰𝔬𝔯'𝔰 𝔥𝔦𝔰-
> 𝔱𝔬𝔯𝔶; 𝔟𝔲𝔱 𝔬𝔫𝔩𝔶 𝔰𝔬𝔪𝔢 𝔪𝔬𝔯𝔢 𝔬𝔯 𝔩𝔢𝔰𝔰 𝔣𝔞𝔫𝔱𝔞𝔰𝔱𝔦𝔠
> 𝔄𝔡𝔲𝔪𝔟𝔯𝔞𝔱𝔦𝔬𝔫, 𝔰𝔶𝔪𝔟𝔬𝔩𝔦𝔠𝔞𝔩𝔩𝔶, 𝔭𝔢𝔯𝔥𝔞𝔭𝔰 𝔰𝔦𝔤-
> 𝔫𝔦𝔣𝔦𝔠𝔞𝔫𝔱𝔩𝔶 𝔢𝔫𝔬𝔲𝔤𝔥, 𝔰𝔥𝔞𝔡𝔬𝔴𝔦𝔫𝔤 𝔣𝔬𝔯𝔱𝔥 𝔱𝔥𝔢
> 𝔰𝔞𝔪𝔢! 〰〰〰〰〰〰〰〰〰〰〰

LIST OF ILLUSTRATIONS.

𝕱𝖎𝖗𝖘𝖙 𝖔𝖋 𝖆𝖑𝖑 𝖆 𝖌𝖔𝖔𝖉 𝕻𝖔𝖗𝖙𝖗𝖆𝖎𝖙 𝖎𝖋 𝖘𝖚𝖈𝖍 𝖊𝖝𝖎𝖘𝖙𝖘;
𝖋𝖆𝖎𝖑𝖎𝖓𝖌 𝖙𝖍𝖆𝖙, 𝖊𝖛𝖊𝖓 𝖆𝖓 𝖎𝖓𝖉𝖎𝖋𝖋𝖊𝖗𝖊𝖓𝖙 𝖎𝖋
𝖘𝖎𝖓𝖈𝖊𝖗𝖊 𝖔𝖓𝖊. 𝕹𝖊𝖝𝖙 𝖎𝖓 𝖉𝖎𝖗𝖊𝖈𝖙𝖓𝖊𝖘𝖘
𝖆𝖗𝖊 𝖆 𝖒𝖆𝖓'𝖘 𝖌𝖊𝖓𝖚𝖎𝖓𝖊
𝕷𝖊𝖙𝖙𝖊𝖗𝖘.

I. Old Chelsea.

GREAT CHEYNE ROW was built in 1708, four years before William, the last of the Chelsea Lord Cheynes, left the "Place" or "Manor House" and returned to his Buckinghamshire seat.

Building of Cheyne Row.

In 1706 Lord Cheyne bought from John Lawrence, heir-apparent to the property, "Three messuages and gardens on the North side of Lordship Yard," and it was probably on part of this land that the terrace or "Row" was built a year or two later.

An earlier date has been ascribed to Carlyle's house in Cheyne Row, which has been written of as a seventeenth-century dwelling; and with a view to clearing up this point I have referred to an extremely valuable and interesting manuscript to which I was fortunate enough to have access. This is a description of the Parish of Chelsey and a Terrier of the Glebe and other lands, with maps and particulars of acreage and ownership,

B

written by Dr. King, who was Rector of Chelsea from 1694 to
1732.

In the map of this portion of the Parish, which was drawn by him
in 1694 (and, it appears, corrected up to a later date), the present
site of Cheyne Row forms part of a " Bowling Green and Garden,
belonging to the Three Gunns; " while " Lord Cheyne's House,
Gardens, Courts, Yards, and 3 closes, 18 acres, 3 roods, 31
poles " lie just to the south, and " Mr. Woodcock's Long Garden "
eastward, behind.

With this delightful and precious volume, which has never been
published, before me, I could not resist transcribing the good
Doctor's prefatory account of his Parish; and it may be of
interest to quote part of it here, that visitors to the Chelsea of
to-day may gain some idea of the Village of Palaces of two
centuries ago.

A description
of Chelsea
when Cheyne
Row was built.

" Chelsey," he begins, " is a sweet and pleasant village situated
on the North side of the Noble River Thames next to Westminster. It is bounded on the East by a little rivulet which runs into
the Thames, and divides it from St. Martin's in the Fields, on the
West by another Rivulet which runs also into the Thames and
separates it from Fulham; on the South it is bounded by the
River Thames and on the North by the Parish of Kensington, from
which it divided for the most part by the Great Road or Highway
which leads from Fulham, Wallom Green thro' Knightsbridge to
London.

"The Town stands upon a gentle rising ground or Hill about
15 feet higher than the River which makes the Cellars and
Kitchens which are underground dry, clean and healthy. And
this advance of situation affords a most pleasant and delightfull
prospect on the East towards London and Westminster w^{c}h are
in full view; Northward to Kensington, Hampstead and Highgate
and on the South into Kent and Surrey. The soil is generally

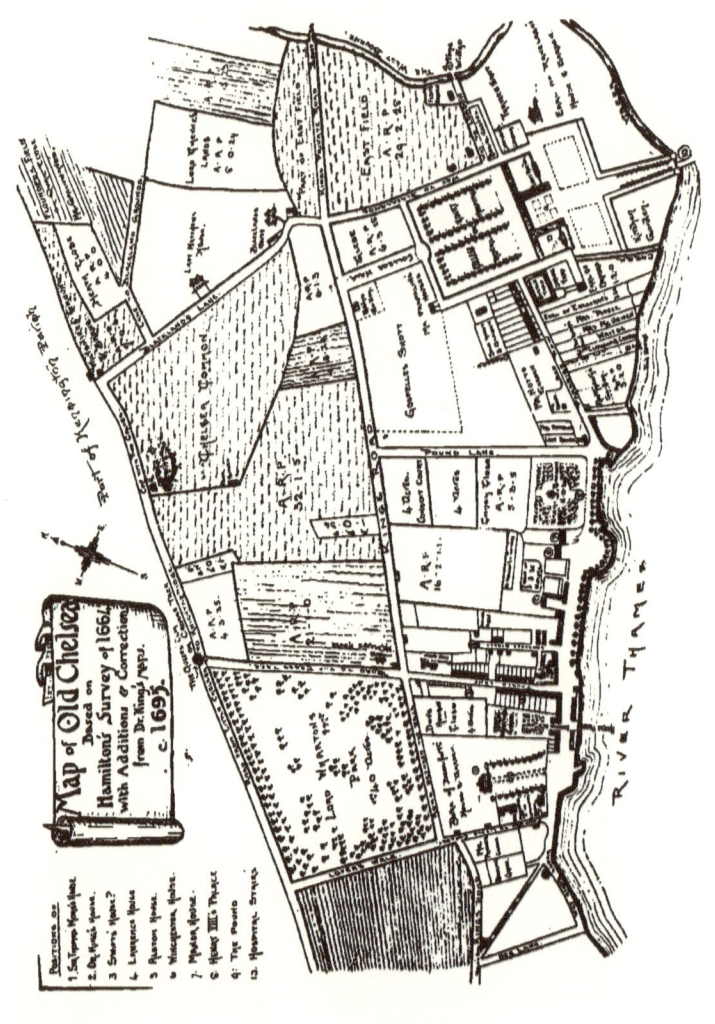

within 6 inches of the surface sand and gravell the Shoar along the Thames is all gravell and Pebbles wch renders it so neat and clean that as soon as the tide is out it affords a clean walk to take Boat. And Mr. Cambden is of opinion that it had name of Chelsey (wch is sometimes written Chelsea or Chelshith) from a Shelf or Bed of Sands or Gravell in the River of wch several are to be seen at low water.

" To this openess of view, pleasantness of situation and dryness of soil succeeds another advantage of a most Healthy air with wch this noble village is blessed in a very eminent manner. Insomuch that no village in the neighbourhood of London contributes more to the ease or recovery of Physical Astmatical and Consumptive Persons or is more resorted to for that purpose than Chelsey.

" Upon account of the forementioned great conveniences and advantages with wch this fair vill is dignified it has the Honor to be inhabited by divers of the Nobility and Gentry of the first Quality and Rank. And this a Privilege she has enjoyed for several generations."

Such was the pet resort of fashion and of rank in which Cheyne Row was built. Its rapidly increasing popularity is attested by Bowack's record, that while in 1664 it had only thirty or forty houses, in 1705 it numbered 300 within its bounds.

The Writer of a Book, is not he a Preacher preaching not to this Parish or that, on this day or that, but to all men in all times and places?

Does the Hebrew People prophetically sing
"Ou' clo'!" in all thoroughfares these
eighteen hundred years in vain? ∿∿∿

II. Cheyne Row.

Early tenants of Cheyne Row.

OF the eighteenth-century tenants of Cheyne Row we have not traced any interesting records. John Hall, historical engraver to George III., dwelt there, 1769-74; John Denyer, collector of books, was also an inhabitant. One genuine but very humble entry of honest toil was, indeed, discovered while the house was under repair. Laboriously scratched on a pane in the upper sash of Mrs. Carlyle's bedroom window is the following :—" John Harbet Knowles cleaind all the windows in this house and painted part in the 18 year of age March 7. 1794." So Carlyle's work of enlightenment at Cheyne Row had its modest precursor there in the year before his birth.

Past and present in the Row.

The block of a dozen houses forming Cheyne Row proper has undergone various changes since they were built, nearly 190 years ago. The broad Greek-patterned eave cornices have disappeared except on two or three of the houses. The red-tiled roofs have given place to slate-sided mansard rooms. The beautiful porticos, apse-shaped, triangular and square, survive on three of the street doors only. The sunk areas have been deepened, the

CHEYNE ROW (1895).

narrow fourth windows closed; the broad mouldings of the
original four-paned sashes (which remain in some of the back
windows of Carlyle's House) have been replaced by the meagre
framework of a later day; the green painted venetian outside
shutters, too, have vanished. Orange House, the beautiful old
tenement in its walled garden which headed the Row, has been
demolished for the erection of a big Catholic church which spoils
the charm and proportion of the façade, and has certainly con-
tributed nothing appropriate in its place. The large pollard
limes have succumbed, though younger trees succeed them; and
a dingy block of Peabody Dwellings has arisen behind the brick
wall opposite.

And yet, though much of its delight has been irretrievably
marred, something of its old-world pleasant picturesqueness remains. The vista of irregular fronts, trending down to the
Embankment garden and the river beyond, has still its quiet
charm; and when spring brings the glint of green leaves, and
sunshine warms the tone of brick or tile, gleams on the white
porches, and casts here and there its lines and masses of shadow,
the little street claims place among the lovable by-ways of a
fascinating quarter.

It was in February, 1834, that some last straw of domestic *The Carlyles*
worry at Craigenputtock turned the balance finally in favour of *move to
London.*
the Carlyles' long-contemplated move to London. The next two
months were spent in "burning the ships;"—disposing of some
part of their stock and belongings; and in May Carlyle hurried
up to his old lodgings at 4, Ampton Street, to begin his house-
hunting. "Leigh Hunt," he writes, "talked much about a quite
delightful house he had (for ten children too) at Chelsea, all
wainscoted, etc., for 30 guineas," and to Chelsea accordingly he
made his way.

The first survey of Dr. King's "sweet and pleasant village"

did not, it seems, attract him, but after searching Brompton, Kensington, and Regent's Park neighbourhoods " till his feet were lamed under him," he returned to see a house which Hunt had discovered for him, some fifty yards from his own " gipsy " establishment at 4, Upper Cheyne Row.

Paradise to All and Sundry. My friends,
I think you are much mistaken about
Paradise! " No Paradise for any-
body: he that cannot do without
Paradise go his ways:" suppose you tried that for
a while! I reckon
that the safer
version.

III. "No. 5."

CARLYLE was much taken with "No. 5, Great Cheyne Row," on his next visit. He went again. "At each new visit your opinion gets a little hitch the contrary way from its former tendency. Imagination has outgone the reality. I nevertheless still feel a great liking for this excellent old house. Chelsea is unfashionable : it was once the resort of the Court and great, however; hence numerous old houses in it at once cheap and excellent;"—an amusing appendix to Dr. King's earlier encomium.

First accounts of "No. 5."

A third visit resulted in the following charming description of the house and its surroundings—his future home for nearly half a century.

"The street runs down upon the river, which I suppose you might see by stretching out your head from the front window, at a distance of fifty yards on the left. We are called 'Cheyne Row' proper (pronounced *Chainie* Row) and are a genteel neighbourhood; two old ladies on one side, unknown character on the other, but with 'pianos.' The street is flag-pathed, sunk storied, iron railed, all old-fashioned and tightly done up; looks

Carlyle's description of the house.

out on a rank of sturdy old *pollarded* (that is, beheaded) lime-
trees standing there like giants in *tawtie* wigs (for the new
boughs are still young); beyond this a high brick wall; back-
wards a garden, the size of our back one at Comley Bank, with
trees, etc., in bad culture; beyond this, green hayfields and tree
avenues, once a bishop's pleasure grounds, an unpicturesque yet
rather cheerful outlook. The house itself is eminent, antique,
wainscoted to the very ceiling, and has been all new painted and
repaired; broadish stair with massive balustrade (in the old
style); corniced and as thick as one's thigh; floors thick as a
rock, wood of them here and there worm-eaten, yet capable of
cleanness, and still with thrice the strength of a modern floor.

"And then as to rooms, Goody! Three stories beside the
sunk story, in every one of them three apartments, in depth
something like forty feet in all—a front dining-room (marble
chimney-piece, etc.), then a back dining-room or breakfast-room,
a little narrower by reason of the kitchen stairs; then, out of this
and narrower still (to allow a back window, you consider), a
china-room or pantry, or I know not what, all shelved and fit to
hold crockery for the whole street. Such is the ground area,
which of course continues to the top, and furnishes every bedroom with a dressing-room or second bedroom; on the whole a
most massive, roomy, sufficient old house with places, for example,
to hang, say, three dozen hats or cloaks on, and as many crevices
and queer old presses and shelved closets (all light and new
painted in their way) as would gratify the most covetous Goody
—rent, thirty-five pounds!

"I confess I am strongly tempted. Chelsea is a singular
heterogeneous kind of spot, very dirty and confused in some
places, quite beautiful in others, abounding in antiquities and
the traces of great men—Sir Thomas More, Steele, Smollett, etc.
Our row, which for the last three doors or so is a street, and

CARLYLE AND "NERO" IN THE BACK COURT (1857).

none of the noblest, runs out upon a 'Parade' (perhaps they call it[1]) running along the shore of the river, a broad highway with huge shady trees, boats lying moored, and a smell of shipping and tar. Battersea Bridge (of wood[2]), a few yards off; the broad river with white-trowsered, white-shirted Cockneys dashing by like arrows in their long canoes of boats; beyond, the green, beautiful knolls of Surrey with their villages.—On the whole a most artificial green painted, yet lively, fresh, almost opera-looking business, such as you can fancy. Finally, Chelsea abounds more than any place in omnibi, and they take you to Coventry Street for sixpence. Revolve all this in thy fancy and judgment, my child, and see what thou canst *make* of it."

Mrs. Carlyle came up to London a week or two later to see with her own eyes what she could make of it, for her husband had felt that she should come and take a share in the momentous decision. "Unless you specially order it no final arrangement shall be made till we both make it," he wrote; "ought not my little *coagitor* to have a vote herself in the choice of an abode that is to be *ours*?" She joined Carlyle at his Ampton Street lodging, was taken by him to see the three or four abodes which had pleased him best in his previous explorations, and soon cast her vote decisively in favour of Cheyne Row. *Mrs. Carlyle arrives in town.*

Three days later they took possession. Here is Carlyle's account: "Tuesday 10th of June, 1834, was the day of our alighting, amidst heaped furniture in this house where we were to continue for life. I well remember bits of the drive from Ampton Street: what damp-clouded kind of sky it was; how in crossing Belgrave Square Chico,[3] whom *she* had brought from Craigenputtock in her lap, burst out into singing, which we all (Bessy Barnet sat with us in the old hackney coach) strove *Taking possession.*

---

[1] Cheyne Walk.   [2] Alas, no more.   [3] The canary.

C.

to accept as a promising omen. The business of sorting and settling with two or three good carpenters, already on the ground, was at once gone into with boundless alacrity, and under such management as hers went on at a mighty rate; even the three or four days of quasi camp life or gipsy life, had a kind of gay charm to us; and hour by hour we saw the confusion abating— growing into victorious order. Leigh Hunt was continually send- ing us notes; most probably would in person step across before bedtime and give us an hour of the prettiest melodious discourse. In about a week, it seems to me, all was swept and garnished, fairly habitable, and continued incessantly to get itself polished, civilized, and beautiful to a degree that surprised me."

In the " Reminiscences " he adds:

"Her arrival I best of all remember: ah me! she was clear for *this* poor house (which she gradually, as poverty a little withdrew after long years of pushing, has made so beautiful and comfortable) in preference to all my other samples: and here we spent our two and thirty years of hard battle against fate, hard but not quite unvictorious, when she left me as in her car of heaven's fire. My noble one! I say deliberately, her part in the stern battle, and except myself none knows how stern, was brighter and braver than my own."

A noble Fight at my side; a valiant strang-
ling of serpents day after day done gaily
by her (for most part) as I had
to do it angrily and gloomily;
thus we went on
together. Ay
de mi!

THE GARDEN, FROM THE BACK DINING-ROOM WINDOW.

Only the noble lift willingly with their whole strength. ∿∿∿∿∿∿

IV. The Garden.

BUT Carlyle took his part in the work of settling in. He hung his favourite pictures and prints in the front first floor room, which was to be his study; he went (with his wife) to "some dim ironmonger's" to buy kettles and pans and a "tinder-box with steel and flint, which was part of our outfit (incredible as it may seem at this date); I could myself burn rags into tinder, and I have groped my way to the kitchen, in sleepless nights, to strike a light for my pipe in that manner." He started vigorously to weed and re-make the borders, and set the slips of jessamine and gooseberry which had been brought from "Puttock." This poor overgrown strip of back garden, indeed, saw a good deal of the new tenant of No. 5, and the picture of Collins the gardener in Sterling's "Onyx Ring" is no doubt drawn from Carlyle, whom in later years Mrs. Allingham has also charmingly depicted seated against its wall with his cat Tib.

Sometimes he would "delve, to compose himself," after some long devastating struggle with the "Cromwell," or the "Frederick;" sometimes, in the hot weather, he would bring his writing-table and papers out into a shady corner and work there; sometimes, too, when all hope of sleep forsook him, he would creep downstairs in his dressing-gown, grope his way to the tinder-box on the kitchen mantelshelf, light the long clay pipe, and sit the night out in the little stone-flagged court, till before him, eastward behind the trees and the roofs and gleam of London, the great dawn streamed up once more. He was fond of this secluded little back court, where in summer an awning was sometimes stretched; here, with a watering-pot to cool the flags, his writing-table, and a butler's tray full of books at his side, he could work when heat drove him from his sublime double-walled garret. There is a quaint account in one letter to his wife of his " swashing this pavement with a scrub-brush and ten or twelve pails of water into some degree of tolerability," and finding it decidedly hard work for three-quarters of an hour.

The back court.

One of his earliest purchases in London was a set of garden tools. " I will soon give it at least a clean face," he writes to his mother; and adds: " It is of admirable comfort to me in the smoking way. I can wander about in dressing-gown and straw hat in it as of old, and take my pipe in peace." Indeed, for a London garden, it was not unproductive; for besides the jessamine and vines, there were a rose-bush or two, a cherry-tree which bore fruit after its kind, a walnut-tree, from which Mrs. Carlyle gathered nearly sixpence worth of walnuts, plum-tree blossom, wallflowers, and much spear-mint. Here stood the quaint china barrels often referred to in Mrs. Carlyle's letters as " noblemen's seats." The sweetbriar sent from Scotland by Mrs. Russell, from Holmhill, did not survive. " It hurried itself," Mrs. Carlyle declared, " to put out leaves when it should have been quietly taking root; a procedure not confined to sweetbriars; one sees human beings go off in the same fashion."

Fruit after its kind.

When paint and workmen made the house intolerable, Mrs. Carlyle would raise her tabernacle here—consisting of a curtain-

EASTWARD VIEW, FROM AN UPPER WINDOW AT 5, CHEYNE ROW (1857).
CARLYLE READING UNDER THE AWNING.

pole, the library crumb-cloth, and a clothes-line, and read or write beneath it, till, with some unruly gust, it collapsed upon her head. At the farther end, near the wall, is the grave of Nero, her devoted and beloved little dog-companion of many years; but the stone, engraved with his name, has disappeared.

It is to this same wall, by the way, that Carlyle refers in " Shooting Niagara : "

" Nothing I know of is more lasting than a well-made brick. We have them here, at the head of this garden (wall once of a manor park), which are in their third or fourth century (Henry Eighth's time, I was told) and still perfect in every particular."

Always there is a black spot in our sunshine; it is even, as I said, the Shadow of Ourselves.

V. Surroundings.

BUT to return to Carlyle's accounts of the new home
and its neighbourhood:
"We lie safe at a bend of the river, away from all the
great roads, have air and quiet hardly inferior to Craigenputtock,
an outlook from the back windows into mere leafy regions with
here and there a red high-peaked old roof looking through;
and see nothing of London except by day the summits of
St. Paul's Cathedral and Westminster Abbey, and by night the
gleam of the great Babylon affronting the peaceful skies. . . . The
house itself is probably the best we have ever lived in—a right
old strong, roomy brick-house, built near 150 years ago, and
likely to see three races of their modern fashionables fall before
it comes down. It has all been put in perfect repair, and has
closets and conveniences without end. Our furniture suits it
too, being all of a strong, weighty sort."

And again:

Old Dutch-
looking
Chelsea.

"The house pleases us much; it is in the remnant of genuine
old Dutch-looking Chelsea; looks out mainly into trees. We
might see at half a mile's distance Bolingbroke's Battersea;
could shoot a gun into Smollett's old house (at this very time
getting pulled down), where he wrote 'Count Fathom,' and was

wont every Saturday to dine a company of hungry authors and then set them fighting together. Don Saltero's coffee-house still looks as brisk as in Steele's time ; Nell Gwynne's boudoir, still bearing her name, has become a gin-temple (not inappropriately); in fine, Erasmus lodged with More (they say) in a spot not five hundred yards from this. We are encompassed with a cloud of witnesses, good, bad, and indifferent." [1]

Carlyle attributed the cheapness of the house (he paid £35 a year, and I believe the rent was never raised) to our old friend "Gigmanity" (his name for snobbish gentility). "Chelsea is unfashionable ; it is also reputed unhealthy. The former quality we rather like (for our neighbours still are all polite-living people), the latter we do not in the faintest degree believe in, remembering that Chelsea was once considered the London Montpelier."

Carlyle's wonderful eye for the pictorial, and his exquisitely sympathetic gift of word-painting, could not fail to catch and crystallize the subtle charms of Chelsea :

A river-side impression.

"It was towards sunset" (he writes to his brother in August, 1840) "when I first got into the air. Avoiding crowds and highways, I went along Battersea Bridge, and thence by a wondrous path across cowfields, mud ditches, river embankments, over a waste expanse of what attempted to pass for country, wondrous enough in the darkening dusk, especially as I had never been there before, and the very road was uncertain. Boat people sat drinking about the Red House ; steamers snorting about the river, each with a lantern at its nose. Old women sat in strange cottages trimming their evening fire. Bewildered-looking, mysterious coke furnaces glowed at one place, I know

---

[1] The site of More's house is shown on the map of Old Chelsea, p. 3 ; those of Saltero, Smollett, Leigh Hunt, and many others of interest, on the later map, p. 48.

not why. Windmills stood silent. Blackguards, improper
females, and miscellanies sauntered, harmless all. Chelsea
lights burnt many-hued, bright over the water in the distance—
under the great sky of silver, under the great still twilight.
So I wandered full of thoughts, or of things I could not
think."

A marvellous pen-picture, recalling to us those brush-impres-
sions of the self-same scenes at a later day, recorded by one
who was also long a sojourner in Chelsea, and who gave thence
to the world its most characteristic portrait of Carlyle.[1]

Doubts.   At times indeed, when the recurrent moods of desperate
depression and dissatisfaction were upon him, he doubted the
wisdom of his migration to London.

---

[1] It recalls, too, another exquisite bit of descriptive writing, which, as
conveying the impressions of Carlyle's earlier home, I cannot refrain from
quoting. It occurs in a letter to John Sterling, written from Scotsbrig in
July, 1837, whither he had fled for rest, broken down by the exertion of
the lectures and the long strain of monetary anxieties which had begotten
them :

"There is no idler, sadder, quieter, more *ghostlike* man in the world
even now than I. . . . Men's very sorrows, and the tears one's heart
weeps when the eye is dry, what is in that either? In an hour, will not
death make it all still again? Nevertheless the old brook—Middlebie
burn we call it—still leaps into its '*caudron*' here, gushes clear as crystal
through the chasms and dingles of its '*Linn*,' singing me a song with
slight variations of score these several thousand years—a song better for
me than Pasta's ! I look on the sapphire of St. Bees Head and the Solway
mirror from the gable window. I ride to the top of Blaweery and see all
round from Ettrick Pen to Helvellyn, from Tyndale and Northumberland
to Cairnsmuir and Ayrshire. *Voir c'est avoir.* A brave old earth after
all, in which, as above said, I am content to acquiesce without quarrel,
and, at lowest, hold my peace. One night, late, I rode through the
village where I was born. The old kirkyard tree, a huge old gnarled ash,
was nestling itself softly against the great twilight in the north. A star or
two looked out, and the old graves were all there, and my father and my
sister ; and God was above us all."

THE BACK OF CARLYLE'S HOUSE (1895).

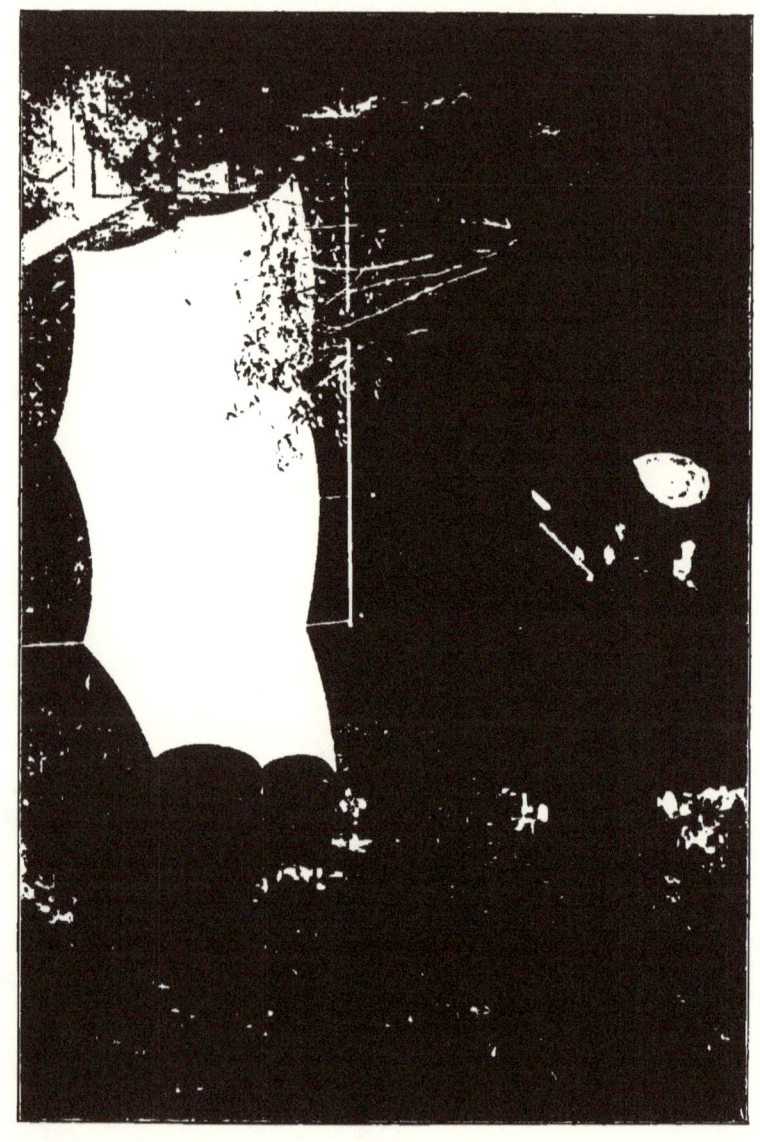

CARLYLE SMOKING UNDER THE AWNING IN THE GARDEN (JULY, 1857).

"I stay here because I am here, and see not, on the whole, where I could get forward with my work much better. Perhaps I shall verily fly to Craigenputtock again before long. Yet I know what solitude is, and imprisonment among black cattle and peat bogs. The truth is, we are never right as we are. 'Oh! the devil burn it,' said the Irish drummer, flogging his countryman, 'there's no pleasing of you, strike where one will.'" But Carlyle gradually realized that the worst demons which beset and tormented him were from within—inescapable ; that their black shadow would mount behind him, go whither he would ; and so, though opportunities presented themselves at intervals, and friends (notably Harriet Martineau) sometimes urged a retreat to the desert, he gradually relinquished all practical ideas of such a move, of which his wife had never approved. Once for all, they had burnt their ships.

"Last night " (he notes in June, 1838), "I sat down to smoke in my night-shirt in the backyard. It was one of the beauti- *A night-watch.* fullest nights ; the half-moon, clear as silver, looked out as from eternity, and the great dawn was streaming up. I felt a remorse, a kind of shudder at the fuss I was making about a sleepless night ; about my sorrow at all, with a life so soon to be absorbed into the great mystery above and around me. Oh! let us be patient."

Though he sometimes appeared unappreciative, and was often lacking in expression of what he felt ("You didn't want praise for merely doing your duty?" Mrs. Carlyle quotes him as saying, adding delightfully, "But I did, though!") there is ample evidence that Carlyle did notice and delight in his wife's constant efforts to make and keep their home comfortable, tasteful, attractive. "No such house," he notes on one of her early letters, "for beautiful thrift, quiet, spontaneous, nay, as it were unconscious—minimum of money reconciled to human comfort *Carlyle's appreciation of his house.*

D

and human dignity—have I anywhere seen where I have been;"
and he speaks of the evenings in their "long, dim-lighted,
perfectly neat and quaint room," as "altogether human and
beautiful; perhaps the best I anywhere had before or since."

𝔚𝔥𝔞𝔱 𝔄𝔠𝔱 𝔬𝔣 𝔏𝔢𝔤𝔦𝔰𝔩𝔞𝔱𝔲𝔯𝔢 𝔴𝔞𝔰 𝔱𝔥𝔢𝔯𝔢 𝔱𝔥𝔞𝔱
𝔱𝔥𝔬𝔲 𝔰𝔥𝔬𝔲𝔩𝔡𝔰𝔱 𝔟𝔢 𝔥𝔞𝔭𝔭𝔶? 𝔚𝔥𝔞𝔱 𝔦𝔣
𝔱𝔥𝔬𝔲 𝔴𝔢𝔯𝔱 𝔟𝔬𝔯𝔫 𝔞𝔫𝔡 𝔭𝔯𝔢𝔡𝔢𝔰𝔱𝔦𝔫𝔢𝔡
𝔫𝔬𝔱 𝔱𝔬 𝔟𝔢 𝔥𝔞𝔭𝔭𝔶, 𝔟𝔲𝔱 𝔱𝔬 𝔟𝔢
𝔘𝔫𝔥𝔞𝔭𝔭𝔶! 𝔆𝔩𝔬𝔰𝔢 𝔱𝔥𝔶
𝔅𝔶𝔯𝔬𝔫, 𝔬𝔭𝔢𝔫 𝔱𝔥𝔶
𝔊𝔬𝔢𝔱𝔥𝔢.

CORNER IN DRAWING-ROOM (1881), WITH CARLYLE'S READING CHAIR,
GIVEN HIM BY JOHN FORSTER.

> Cosmos is not Chaos simply by this one
> quality, that it is governed. ✦✦✦✦✦✦

VI. The Order of the Day.

THE *ménage* at Cheyne Row underwent so many vicissitudes that it is difficult to give any clear account of it. .
Breakfast—at which letters were looked for to
"scatter the misanthropy we are both given to at the beginning of
the day, like other nervous people who have bad nights"—breakfast was oftenest taken in the little back dining-room, or
morning-room, with its window overlooking the garden; and then
Carlyle would go off upstairs to his books and work, while his wife
descended to the dark, stone-paved, open-ranged kitchen, with
which so much of the worrying "cares of bread" that often
clouded her days was associated.

During the earlier years of their tenancy, the pleasant three-
windowed room on the first floor was Carlyle's study. Here, he
wrote : "I have got my little book-press set up, my table fixed
firm in its place; and sit here awaiting what Time and I in our
questionable wrestle shall make out between us." Here the
"French Revolution" was written; it was here that Mill,
"pale as Hector's ghost," begging Mrs. Carlyle to go down and
speak to some one in his carriage at the door, broke to her
husband the destruction of the manuscript of the first volume, of
which the story has been so often told. Here, when later on it

[margin: Breakfast.]

[margin: The drawing-room.]

became the drawing-room, was the scene of those evening gatherings to which so many notable and interesting people came, and of which something must presently be said. Here, parallel with the windows, head towards the fireplace, stood the large red chintz-covered sofa on which Mrs. Carlyle was doomed to spend so much of her life. It was here that Tyndall's telegram [1] was brought her on the evening of the Edinburgh Address, leading to that little scene of joyous enthusiasm of which it is hard to read the account without the feeling of tears; ending in the sudden fainting collapse which told of the anxious strain that had preceded it. And here, finally,—for his bed had been moved into this warm and cheerier room in his last illness—

Where Carlyle died.

with his wife's work-table and trinkets, which had been kept in their places since her death, close to his hand, on the morning of the 5th of February, 1881, Thomas Carlyle died.

It is a room, indeed, charged with tragic and distinguished memories, the psychic influence of which no desolation, however profound, has been able to destroy.

Books.

As books accumulated, bookcases were fitted in the recesses to right and left of the mantelpiece, and a larger one, nine feet wide, and reaching nearly to the ceiling, filled the wall opposite the fireplace.[2] Carlyle's writing-table, which stood here in earliest

The writing-table.

and latest years, he bequeathed to Sir James Stephen, in whose family it remains. "I know," he wrote in his will, "he will accept it as a distinguished mark of my esteem. He knows that it belonged to my honoured father-in-law and his daughter, and that I have written all my books upon it except only Schiller, and that for the fifty years and upwards that are now passed I have considered it among the most precious of my possessions."

[1] "A perfect triumph."
[2] This was removed from the drawing-room to give space for the large oil-painting called "The Little Drummer."

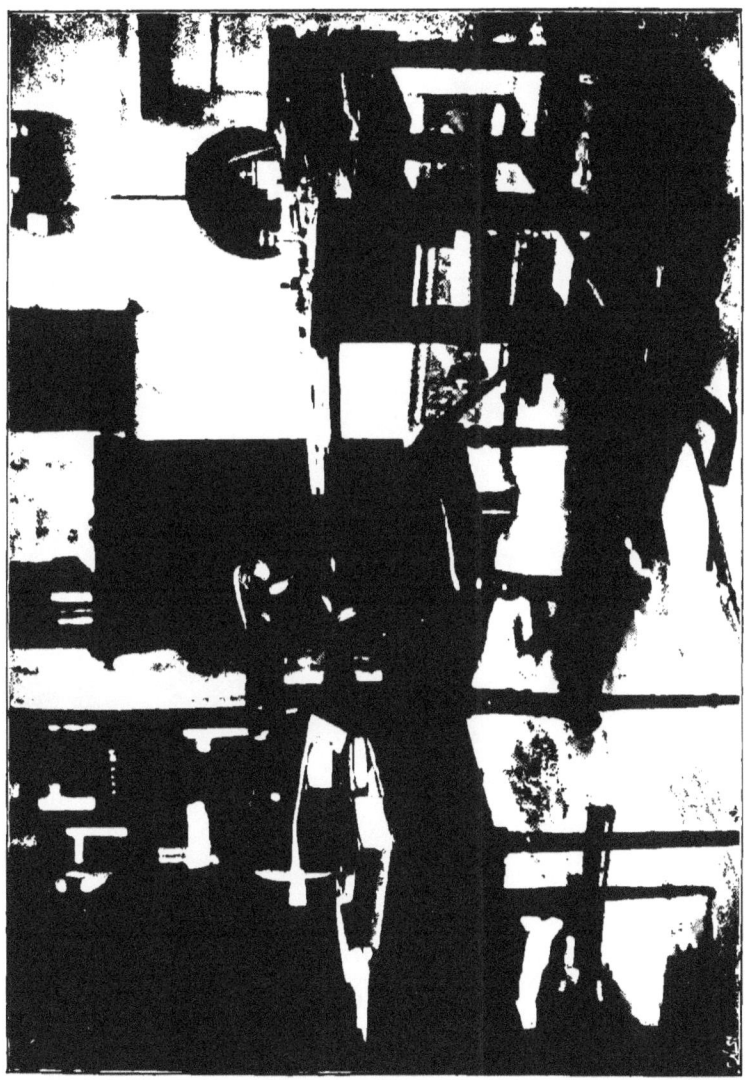

THE GARRET STUDY (1857). CARLYLE'S WRITING-DESK AND CHAIR.

His pens were often a sore trial to him. He found himself obliged "Scriptory ware." to abandon quills, and take to "iron pens;" but their irritating vagaries often brought anathema on their makers, as did the "'cheap and nasty' system which has prevailed in regard to paper and ink everywhere for twenty years; worse to me almost than the loss of an arm."[1] Yet his writing—until late years, when the tremulous motion of that hardly-used right hand began, which eventually made work with it impossible—was beautiful in clearness and character ; and though Miss Martineau tells a humorous story of an Annan printer's terror of his copy,[2] later manuscripts are models of legibility and precision.

In 1853 the plague of the neighbouring cocks—"the demon The soundless room. fowls"—reached a climax, and the much-debated sound-proof room was built at the top of the house. Here, in place of a couple of garrets in the roof, Carlyle had raised (at a cost, in all, of nearly £200) a spacious square chamber, with inner partitions, front and back, forming a double wall against the outside world. Outer windows and inner doors were made for ventilation, but the room was lighted entirely from above, a large skylight, with sliding shutters beneath, occupying most of the roof-space. Here, then, "whirled aloft by angry elements," he took refuge with his work, and here he completed what Dr. Garnett has well named his "thirteen years' war with Frederick." At first the costly experi- "Friedrich." ment seemed successful. The light was superb, "all softer sounds were killed, and of sharp sounds scarce the thirtieth part could penetrate." But this satisfaction was short-lived. The thing was, as his keen eye had at once detected, "jerry-built," "Satan's invisible world exposed." "mere work of Belial, father of lies." In winter he was frozen

---

[1] In later times he used, with approval, Perry and Co.'s "Balance Spring Pen No. 140, medium point."

[2] Not because of the writing, but because of the many alterations he generally made in the "revises."

there ; the patent miracle of a fireplace gave no heat, and his wife went off to Bramah to replace it by one " of a merely human sort, which actually warmed the room." In summer the oppo-site extreme was equally trying, and recourse to the watering-pot was necessary to cool the air about his table, till he was driven down into the garden. However, " it got patched together into something of supportability," and Carlyle continued to occupy it till the long wrestle " in the valley of the shadow of Frederick the Great," as he used to describe it, was over in 1865, when he quitted it for ever, and it became thenceforth the servants' bed-room. From that time onward he wrote—so long as he wrote at all—in the ground-floor room ("thanks to her last service to me, shifting me thither again "), and there the great book-shelf, the bureau, and the other cases and appurtenances of his study found their final place.

" Nero."   I never mount those garret stairs without recalling one charm-ing little reminiscence.   " Nero," the little white Cuban spaniel, came to them in the winter of 1849-50, and during the next ten years before his death (after being run over by a cart), he became a devoted little companion, greatly beloved by Mrs. Carlyle, and gradually endearing himself to her husband, whom he regularly accompanied, to the very end, in his evening rambles. " Once, perhaps in his third year here, he came patter-ing upstairs to my garret ; scratched duly, was let in, and brought me (literally) the *gift of a* HORSE (which I had talked of needing)! Brought me, to wit, a letter hung to his neck, inclosing on a saddler's card the picture of a horse, and adjoined to it her cheque for £50, full half of some poor legacy that had fallen to her."   Carlyle could not accept the gift, but he did get a horse soon afterwards ; and he grew to love the small comrade of his night-walks, " the little dim white speck of life, of love, fidelity, and feeling, girdled by the darkness as of Night eternal ; " and on

THE GARRET STUDY (1857). CARLYLE AT WORK.

"February 1st, 1860," Nero, mercifully put out of pain by Dr. Barnes, was honourably buried at the end of the garden, where a stone, with date and name, long marked the spot.[1]

Dinner was an often-moved feast—shifted from time to time in vain hope of appeasing the dreaded demons of insomnia or dyspepsia, the "raal mental awgony i' my ain inside" to which there are so many grimly jocular allusions. We hear of it at two, at three, at four, at half-past five, at seven; and we recall in Mrs. Carlyle's letters the difficulties, which her nervous weakness no doubt exaggerated, in getting her husband's few possible dishes—his special soup, his quarter of boiled fowl, his pudding—cooked in the one way that he could take them, by a somewhat unfortunate succession of servants. *Dinner.*

A record of Carlyle's home life which made no mention of tobacco would be incomplete indeed. Everybody knows the twenty-inch long churchwarden clays which he habitually smoked. They were made by, and obtained from White's, formerly of the Canongate, Edinburgh (now at Glasgow), and their consignment was not always an easy matter. When Carlyle was starting for Mentone in 1867, he insisted on packing a box of fifty of these delicate pipes in a way which Tyndall, who was at Cheyne Row at the time, declared must lead to certain disaster. Carlyle was obdurate and had his way, but the Professor's revenge was speedy. In a week came an urgent letter from Mentone confessing that of the fifty pipes only three had arrived unbroken, and begging for more, and his friend had the satisfaction of scientifically packing and despatching another half hundred, which arrived without a single breakage. *"Consuming his own smoke."*

The number of long clays used at No. 5 must have been very

---

[1] It was there when Mr. and Mrs. Alexr. Carlyle left in 1882, but has since disappeared.

considerable, and the first costermonger or the milkman who passed the doorstep in the morning could generally count on finding a pipe put out for him there. Carlyle's tobacco jar, and the heavy oblong "cutter" for cake tobacco, are now, I think, with various other relics, at his birthplace, the little Arched House at Ecclefechan, whither Carlyle lovers will hardly fail to make pilgrimage on their northward way.

Riding. Carlyle's walks and rides were generally taken in the late afternoon or evening, when he had worked himself out for the day. His first horse was "Citoyenne" (very delicately presented by Mr. Marshall, of Leeds, in 1839). His second was "Fritz," on whom, during the writing of "Friedrich," he rode "some 30,000 miles, much of it (all the winter part of it) under cloud of night, sun just setting when I mounted." He rode somewhat recklessly, with a loose rein, and thoughts perhaps at Prag or Mollwitz. Fritz was clever and a clean stepper, and "had not been brought up to think that the first duty of a horse was to say something witty;" but the pitcher goes often to the well, and in February, 1863, without warning or cause, he and his rider came smash down, the latter unharmed, but the former breaking his knees, and having to be parted with at once. Lady Ashburton sent a tolerable though less intelligent successor, "Noggs," and the riding continued at intervals till October, 1868, when Miss Bromley's once gallant and glorious " Comet " and he " splashed utterly down, horse and rider fairly tracing out their united profile on the soil of Middlesex, in the Holland House region." This was his last ride; and indeed it is only wonderful that catastrophes had not come oftener, or with worse **Walks.** results. Thenceforward walking—of which he had always done much—became his only exercise. In earlier days Clapham and Wandsworth Commons (where he would sit and smoke among the furze bushes) were often visited; later he would do his five

DRAWING-ROOM, NORTH-WEST CORNER (1881).

or six miles regularly in Hyde Park or Battersea, or about Kensington. He never passed the spot (now altered by the fountains) where his wife was last seen alive, without pausing for awhile in silence, with uncovered head. He carried no umbrella, trusting to the broad-brimmed hat for sufficient protection. He was a very frequent figure in the omnibus, and was well known by drivers and conductors, and often recognized by passengers, seated obliquely in the corner by the door. In his last years he used to drive daily in a fly—to Harrow, Richmond, or Sydenham, or for an hour in Kew Gardens; and his last walks were taken on the broad sweep of Chelsea Embankment, which he reckoned "a real improvement."

Work and exercise over, came the brightest, happiest bit of Carlyle's day.

"Home between five and six, with mud mackintoshes off, and the nightmares locked up for awhile, I tried for an hour's sleep before my (solitary, dietetic, altogether simple) bit of dinner; but first always came up for half an hour to the drawing-room and her; where a bright kindly fire was sure to be burning (candles hardly lit, all in trustful chiaroscuro) and a spoonful of brandy in water with a pipe of tobacco (which I had learned to take sitting on the rug, with my back to the jamb, and door never so little open, so that all the smoke, if I was careful, went up the chimney), this was the one bright portion of my black day. Oh, those evening half-hours, how beautiful and blessed they were. . . . She was oftenest reclining on the sofa; wearied enough, she too, with her day's doings and endurings. But her history, even of what was bad, had such grace and truth, and spontaneous, tinkling melody of a naturally cheerful and loving heart, that I never anywhere enjoyed the like." *The evening half-hour.*

Elsewhere he adds:

"Never again shall I have such melodious, humanly beautiful

half-hours; they were the rainbow of my poor dripping day, and reminded me that there otherwise was a sun."

Again and again Carlyle refers to these half-hours of quiet converse, the one bright point in his dreary days. Two little episodes are particularly memorable; the one where his wife, weakened and exhausted by her prolonged illness, but acting clearly on a preconceived determination, bade him take her place upon the sofa while she took her seat once again at the little piano, and played to him, for the last time, the simple, beloved old Scottish melodies he had always listened to with happiness; the other, when, after the terribly painful period of illness following her accident in Cheapside, the double door to her bedroom was suddenly opened, "and she came limping and stooping on her staff, so gracefully and with such a childlike joy and triumph, to irradiate my solitude."

Bright home, with its bright face, full of love and victorious over all disorder, always shone on me like a star as I journeyed and tumbled along amid the shriekeries and miseries.

A man, be the Heavens ever praised, is sufficient for himself; yet were ten men, united in Love, capable of being and of doing what ten thousand singly would fail in. Infinite is the help man can yield to man.

VII. Guests at Cheyne Row.

THIS twilight half-hour together was sacred to them- Visitors.
selves, and is recalled by Carlyle with delicate
appreciation of the effort his wife made to cheer and
lighten his mood by her brilliantly spun story of the day and
its doings. In the later evening visitors very often joined them,
and it is of these evening hours that friends carried away their
best remembrances.

The list of people, more or less notable, who were admitted to
the lightning play of words and "wits" and Homeric laughter in
that cosy parlour would include most of the names known to
English literature and art in the earlier century. Leigh Hunt, Hunt.
posed like a Lar against the mantelpiece, was often there, from
Upper Cheyne Row in these first days, and continued a visitor for
many years. Erasmus Darwin, "a most diverse kind of mortal,"
early sought them out. John Stuart Mill was Carlyle's closest Mill.
friend in the thirties, but became unfortunately estranged in later
days. Harriet Martineau "of pleasant countenance, full of talk,"
came to arrange about the Lectures to which Carlyle first con-

Sterling.

sented at her instigation. Of the visits of the Sterlings, John, his father, the "Thunderer" (of The Times), and his brother Captain Anthony, we recall the delightful accounts in Carlyle's Life of his friend, whose coming evoked the keenest of intellectual sword-play, "harmless sheet lightning."

Irving.

Edward Irving's one visit he often referred to in later records. "It was in the ground-floor room where I still write. I well recollect his fine chivalrous demeanour to her and how he complimented her, as he well might, on the pretty little room she had made for her husband and self, and running his eyes over her dainty bits of arrangements, ornamentation, all so frugal, simple, full of grace propriety and ingenuity as they were, said smiling, 'You are like an Eve, and make a little Paradise wherever you are.'"

Others of the miscellaneous list of visitors at Cheyne Row were Connop Thirlwall, "the massive Scholar and Sceptic;" Count

D'Orsay.

D'Orsay, the dandy "with an adornment unsurpassable on this planet;" Monckton Milnes, Richard Owen, the naturalist, "a man of real talent and worth, an extremely rare kind of man," Margaret Fuller (afterwards tragically drowned), "full of wit and pathos;" Lord Jeffrey (patron of earlier days), now christened "the Duke of Craigcrook;" Dr. Chalmers, "white-headed, grave, deliberate."

Mazzini.

Of Mazzini's visits and talk we hear more from Mrs. Carlyle than her husband. He was a neighbour and a frequent guest, and the unguarded rashness with which he confided plots and plans contrasts strangely with the excellent calmness and sobriety of his advice when appealed to by her at a very critical epoch. There, too, came Cavaignac, "a fine Bayard soul;" Louis Blanc, "a pretty little miniature of a man;" Charles Gavan Duffy, who found sanctuary at Cheyne Row when his party were tried, exiled, and scattered; and Thomas Erskine, "gentlest, kindest, best bred

THE GROUND FLOOR ROOMS IN 1857.

DRAWN FROM A PHOTOGRAPH OF MR. TAIT'S PICTURE, "AN INTERIOR AT CHELSEA."

of men," with whom at his home at Linlathen Carlyle corresponded regularly.

Other and yet more familiar names need only be enumerated. Charles Kingsley, brought here first, "a delicate boy," by his mother; Dean Stanley, "boring holes in the bottom of the Church of England;" Charles Dickens, "a quiet, shrewd little fellow Dickens. who seems to guess pretty well what he is and what others are;" Arthur Hugh Clough, whose beautiful character and transparent integrity made him a welcome and honoured guest, "a diamond sifted out of the general rubbish heap."

Ralph Waldo Emerson, the valued friend and correspondent of Emerson. so many years, came here first in 1847, and paid his last visit in 1872.

This friendship, which extended—constant in its essence though fluctuating in expression—for more than half a century, was a noble and beautiful feature of the lives of both men, and the collection and publication of the letters which passed between Chelsea and Concord has widened our insight into the character and attitude of each.

Alfred Tennyson came first in July of 1840. Carlyle, returning Tennyson. from his evening walk, found him sitting with Mrs. Carlyle in the little garden, peaceably smoking, and portrayed him faithfully:

"A fine, large-featured, dim-eyed, bronze-coloured, shaggy-headed man is Alfred; dusty, smoky, free and easy. Great now and then when he does emerge (from an inarticulate element of tranquil chaos and tobacco smoke)—a most restful, brotherly, solid-hearted man."

John Ruskin's visits began, it seems, in 1860, though Carlyle Ruskin. and he had long been acquainted. "Full of generous prospective activities" he found him, and in a later letter, after they had seen much of each other, he adds, "Valiant Ruskin seems to me to have the best talent for *preaching* of all men now alive."

In the wilderness he now realized that at least there were *two* voices crying.

Stephen.

Sir James Stephen, "recognisably serious and able, earnest and honest," was another frequent evening visitor.

Huxley.

Froude came first in June, 1849, and thereafter very constantly; Professor Huxley, John Tyndall, Mr. Lecky, John Forster, were among the eminent men who mounted the charming old stairway

Artists.

of No. 5 in the later years. Sir John Millais, Samuel Lawrence, and Mr. Watts essayed to portray its tenant; Edgar Boehm pursued the same difficult, elusive task in other materials; Mr. Whistler achieved a remarkable canvas of the man of whom, in spite—or perhaps because—of the strong, rugged force and character of his features, artists found it so hard to render faithful account.[1]

Amongst later visitors was Lord (then Sir Garnet) Wolseley, who Carlyle hoped might one day be bidden " to lock the door of yonder place (the House of Commons) and turn them all about their business."

A visitor's impressions.

Moncure Conway ("friend of the nigger"), who was much at Cheyne Row in the sixties, gives this among his impressions:

" I cannot repress some bitterness of feeling when I contrast the notion which the world is forming of the home at Chelsea with the memories of it that rise before me. I used to go once or sometimes twice in the week, towards nine in the evening. By that time Carlyle was stretched on the floor [in the drawing-room upstairs] his back cushioned against the wall, the bowl of his long clay pipe in the fireplace, so that the smoke might not disturb his invalid wife. She reclined on the sofa beside him.

[1] "What you ask about *my* likeness," he wrote to Sterling in 1841, " is unanswerable. I likened it four months ago, when I struck work in sitting, to a compound of the head of a demon and of a flayed *horse. Infandum!*"

After greetings their conversation was resumed, and Carlyle went on pouring out such good stories as those treasured in his wife's letters. Mrs. C. took a lively share in the talk with that easy freedom not usual in oppressed wives, and with so much point and sparkle that I sometimes wondered that there were not more clashings between these swords that had got into one sheath. One could not look upon Mrs. Carlyle's face then without reading in it love and reverence for her husband."

About eleven, as the evening drew to a close, was served—at any rate in the earlier years—that "endlessly admirable morsel of Scotch porridge" which Leigh Hunt so admired and enjoyed, and which was Carlyle's particular "nightcap." Porridge.

𝔉𝔦𝔫𝔡 𝔞 𝔪𝔞𝔫 𝔴𝔥𝔬𝔰𝔢 𝔴𝔬𝔯𝔡𝔰 𝔭𝔞𝔦𝔫𝔱 𝔶𝔬𝔲 𝔞 𝔩𝔦𝔨𝔢𝔫𝔢𝔰𝔰, 𝔶𝔬𝔲 𝔥𝔞𝔳𝔢 𝔣𝔬𝔲𝔫𝔡 𝔞 𝔪𝔞𝔫 𝔴𝔬𝔯𝔱𝔥 𝔰𝔬𝔪𝔢𝔱𝔥𝔦𝔫𝔤.

VIII. The Bed-Chambers.

Carlyle's bed-room.

THE chronicle of the nights, alas, is only too ample! Carlyle's bedroom was the back chamber on the second floor; raised and parted from the street, indeed, but overlooking the neighbouring yards, with their dog kennels and hen-coops and other demoniacal possessions. One need not here recall the too plentiful records of the havoc and desolation which these things—and others—dealt with fatal persistence upon two of the most nerve-smitten beings in England. They make gloomy reading of the letters and journals of both, and those who have known what chronic insomnia means have found it the easier to condone much that Carlyle, in the "Memorials" and "Reminiscences," has far too bitterly reproached himself with.

Noctes Caerlienses.

But it is not necessary for this rambling chronicle of their House and House Life to enter further upon a theme to which exaggerated and misleading prominence has elsewhere been given.

Two pictures hung in Carlyle's room for which he had a curious fondness. One was the "Belisarius," a French print of Justinian's general begging alms, which he cherished because the face of a young Roman soldier in it reminded his wife of her father, Dr. Welsh.

The other was his beloved "Segretario Ambulante," a small coloured lithograph of a ragged old man seated behind a board on trestles (a quill in his hand, another behind his ear, and a third in his ink-bottle) plying his trade, the writing of letters at dictation for illiterate passers-by. "He is a delightful fellow," said Carlyle; "shows you Literature in its simplest, quite steadfast condition, below which it *cannot* sink."

The room immediately below Carlyle's, communicating by a double door with the drawing-room, was his wife's bedroom. Here stood the famous red-canopied four-poster bed ; here was the wardrobe she had astonished Mrs. Hunt by painting herself. A little "dressing closet" or bath-room opens out from each of the bedrooms—possibly designed originally for a powdering room for eighteenth-century dames and dandies. The fact that Carlyle's bed was immediately overhead handicapped unnecessarily his wife's slender chances of undisturbed repose ; for when some unruly cock forestalled the morn, she would lie nervously awake expecting the well-known thud above, which meant his desperate abandonment of bed, to try a pipe in the back court, or a walk in the deserted streets, or even a cold bath. *(Mrs. Carlyle' bedroom.)*

That solid, ancient wooden, curtained bed, alas, is perhaps the most typical of all Mrs. Carlyle's belongings. It was brought with their other things from Scotland in 1834. It was her parents' bed at Haddington ;[1] the bed in which she herself was born. In early years at Chelsea she refers with affection to "her own red bed," and looked forward with pleasure to return-

---

[1] This large, elaborate, and very massive bedstead was, it appears, in later years, moved into the spare room, and replaced by a much smaller bed (3 feet 6 inches or 4 feet) ; which, when the house was left in 1882, was given to Mrs. Warren, who had been housekeeper at the time of Mrs. Carlyle's death.

ing to it from her travels; but in later years it was associated
with so much of pain and misery, that at length it became at
times a haunting nightmare, "a sort of red-hot purgatory," in
her overwrought brain. Though destined never here, unhappily,
to witness motherhood again,[1] it was a place of travail—bodily,
mental, spiritual, such as it has been given to few women to
endure for long, and to survive, as she did, bright and unbroken.

Mrs. Carlyle's death.

For here Jane Welsh Carlyle passed into the valley of that
shadow that awaits the weary in their hour of exhaustion. Here
she met and wrestled with those spirits of Darkness whose
promptings have unhinged so many gifted minds. Here she, too,
conquered; and reached, beyond the shadow, a light of eventide
that was almost serenely beautiful and tender. Hither, at last,
her lifeless form was carried on that fatal 21st of April, 1866.
We need but to recall the tragic history, enacted while Carlyle
at Dumfries was resting after the exhaustion of the triumphant
Inaugural Address at Edinburgh. Those of us at least who knew
and revered his wife in Chelsea are not likely to forget the shock of
that Saturday night's tidings; the drive, before her tea party,
in the brougham with old Sylvester on the box; the accident to
the little dog, whom she had put out for a run near Victoria
Gate; the double circle of the drive; the coachman's alarm,
at length, receiving no orders; his appeal to two bystanders at
the park gate, and their terrible verdict; the move to St.
George's Hospital; the anxious conclave at Cheyne Row, where
Froude, Forster, and my father had hurried, as to how the news
should reach Carlyle; his return on the Monday; Tyndall's
visit, and that wonderful, passionate oration, spoken in the

---

[1] "No daughter or son of hers was to sit there," Carlyle wrote of her
little child-chair; "so it had been appointed us .... these [his books]
were our only 'children,' and in a true sense these were verily ours; and
will perhaps live some time in the world, after we are both gone."

MRS. CARLYLE.
DRAWN FROM A PHOTOGRAPH.

drawing-room while she lay still here behind those double doors ; the funeral at Haddington ; the exquisite epitaph on her who was " suddenly snatched away from him, and the light of his life as if gone out."

It may be permitted to close this page of sorrow with an extract from the volumes of Early Letters compiled by Professor Norton.

" The lives of Carlyle and his wife are not represented as they were in this book of Mr. Froude's. There was much that was sorrowful in their experience, much that was sad in their relations to each other. Their mutual love did not make them happy ; did not supply them with the self-control required for happiness. Their faults often prevailed against their love, and ' yet, with a thousand faults, they were both true-hearted people.'

" And through all the dark vicissitudes of life, love did not desert them. Blame each of them as one may, for carelessness, hardness, bitterness, in the course of the years, one reads their lives wholly wrong unless he read in them that the love that had united them was beyond the power of fate and fault to ruin utterly ; that, more permanent than aught else, it abided in the heart of each, and that in what they were to each other it remained the unalterable element."

The front room on this (second) floor was the guest-chamber, or spare room ; a bright, cheerful bedroom, where, besides many members of the Carlyle and Welsh families, James and John Carlyle, Mrs. Carlyle's mother, and others, slept such occasional visitors as Emerson, Gavan Duffy, and many other friends. A touching and characteristic little story is associated with this room. In the spring of 1839, when her mother was staying here, Mrs. Carlyle gave a *soirée*, the first and last of such formal gatherings that was ever undertaken at Cheyne Row.

The spare room.

Mrs. Welsh, anxious that everything should be very nice, bought some additional wax candles and confectionery, which she set out in brilliant array. Her daughter was vexed, thinking there was a look of extravagance about this laden table; she took away some of the cakes, and two of the large wax candles.

FIREPLACE AND CUPBOARD IN SPARE ROOM.

Mrs. Welsh was hurt, and showed it, and Mrs. Carlyle was greatly pained at having wounded her. She wrapped the candles up carefully, and put them away in one of the shelved closets by the fireplace in this spare room. There they remained for seven and twenty years. About a month before her death, Mrs. Carlyle sent for the housekeeper, Mrs. Warren, and confided to her the wish (registered, it seems, on her mother's death in 1842, but mentioned to no one) that when the end came these candles should be lighted and burned at her bedside. This was faithfully remembered and performed, as Carlyle afterwards learned from Mrs. Warren.

In the whole world I had one complete approver; in that, as in other cases, one, and it was worth all.

> **For a genuine man it is no evil to be poor;
> there ought to be Literary Men poor to
> show whether they are genuine or not!**

IX. The "Cares of Bread."

The kitchen.

BUT we must not forget to visit the basement; to go to the foundation of things. What crowding memories from Mrs. Carlyle's letters this spacious "half-sunk" kitchen, with its big, open fireplace, its wooden pump,[1] its racks and dressers, recalls. Great as were the intellectual gifts of its mistress, their brilliancy never dimmed—as with others it usually has—the excellence of her housewifery. Her theory of the management of and relation to those in her service was ideal, though the material vouchsafed her for its accomplishment was poor and disappointing enough. Until quite late years the work that brought Carlyle fame did not bring affluence. For the first twenty years, at least, of their life in Chelsea, his income from his writing probably *averaged* less than £200 a year, though of course it varied greatly from time to time. Mrs. Carlyle had (after her mother's death in 1842) a similar amount from the lease of Craigenputtock, so that their joint income, till nearly 1860, may be taken as under £500 a year, including the interest in savings deposited in the bank at Dumfries.

Thrift.

[1] In relaying the drainage, we came upon the ancient well, deep in the beautiful red Chelsea sand, but long since disused and closed.

The house was always kept in exquisite order, and repairs Housekeep-
and renovations were continually taking place. "The furniture ing.
was simple, but solid and handsome; everything was scrupu-
lously clean, everything good of its kind; and there was an air
of ease, as of a household living within its means. Mr. Carlyle
kept a horse; his wife was always well dressed; they travelled;
they visited; both were open-handed and very generous."
When we consider that all this, and much more, was accom-
plished upon an income so moderate, we need no further
testimony to the housekeeping at No. 5, of which we have a
masterly epitome in the "Budget of a Femme Incomprise,"
elaborated, with trenchant humour, in her letters to Mrs.
Russell.

Such, then, was the home where these two "made out their
questionable struggle." The small things of the great are so
much more interesting than the great things of the small, that
one is tempted to prolong these random recollections.

But enough, it may be hoped, has been given to convey some Shadows.
impression of the home and its life. Those who have gathered
their conception of these from the published letters and memorials,
may miss from the picture something of the pervading shadow
which has there been cast about them with such needless
emphasis. Shadows and sorrows, trouble and suffering there
were, of course, and in full measure. From what human
household are they ever altogether absent? But that most misleading prominence has been given them, by the selection of
letters and extracts published, can hardly be doubted. It is
patent to those who knew them, that both Mr. and Mrs. Carlyle's
descriptions of their doings and endurings in private letters and
journals were strongly coloured by the intensity of the momentary
impression under which they were penned; indeed, they have themselves said as much. Both were nervous folk; both felt things with

the swiftness and energy of an electric flash; both wrote rapidly and unreservedly under the influence of such "feelings;" and wrote, too, with dangerous facility, and the unconquerable instinct of effect.

Reading their story by the clearer light which it yet in part lacks, the calm judgment of time will more and more confirm what those who were privileged to see much of the interior of that home have always testified, that its dark passages have been emphasized out of all proportion with their true place; and that the two noble lives, whose dwelling-place it was, were neither saddened nor embittered in the way, or to the extent, which present prejudice would have us believe.

Man's Unhappiness, as I construe, comes
of his Greatness.

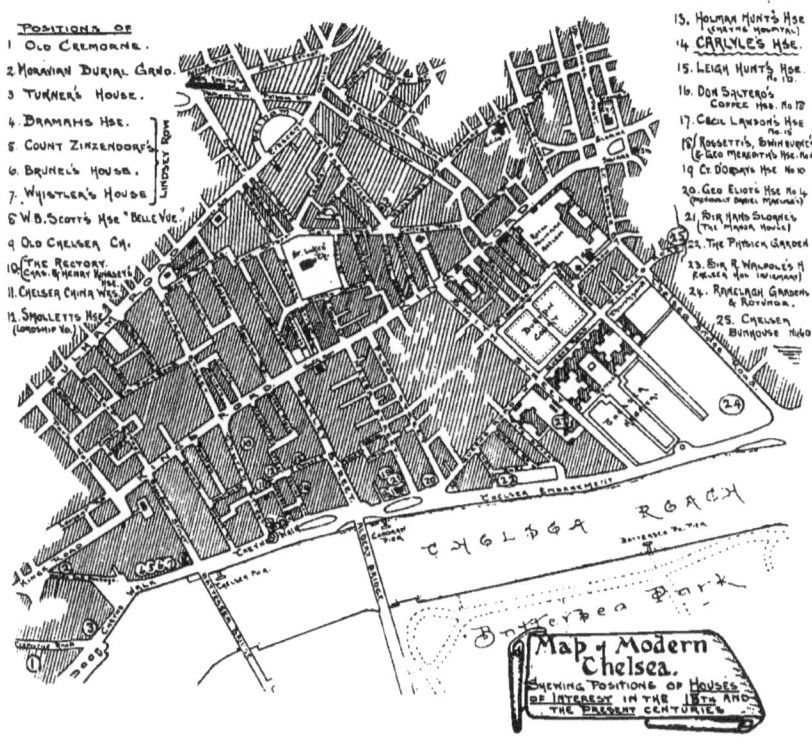

POSITIONS OF

1 OLD CREMORNE.
2 MORAVIAN BURIAL GRND.
3 TURNER'S HOUSE.
4 BRAMAHS HSE.
5 COUNT ZINZENDORF'S
6 BRUNEL'S HOUSE.
7 WHISTLER'S HOUSE
8 W.B.SCOTT'S HSE "BELLEVUE."
9 OLD CHELSEA CH.
10 THE RECTORY. (GRND. BY HENRY KINGSLEY'S HSE.)
11 CHELSEA CHINA WKS.
12 SMOLLETTS HSE (LAWRENCE ST.)

LINDSEY ROW

13 HOLMAN HUNT'S HSE (CHEYNE HOSPITAL)
14 CARLYLE'S HSE.
15 LEIGH HUNT'S HSE.
16 DON SALTERO'S COFFEE HSE. No. 18
17 CECIL LAWSON'S HSE No. 15
18 ROSSETTI'S, SWINBURNE'S & GEO MEREDITH'S HSE. No. 16
19 G. DOBATH'S HSE No. 10
20 GEO ELIOT'S HSE No. 4 (FORMERLY DANIEL MACLISE)
21 SIR HANS SLOANE'S (THE MANOR HOUSE)
22 THE PHYSICK GARDEN
23 SIR R WALPOLE'S H (CHELSEA HOS. INFIRMARY)
24 RANELAGH GARDENS & ROTUNDA.
25 CHELSEA BUNHOUSE No. 60

CHELSEA EMBANKMENT

CHELSEA REACH
BATTERSEA BRIDGE

Battersea Park

Map of Modern
Chelsea.
SHEWING POSITIONS OF HOUSES
OF INTEREST IN THE 18TH AND
THE PRESENT CENTURIES

APPENDICES.

> In the commonest human face there lies
> more than Raphael will take away with him.

LIST OF PICTURES, ETC.

From Notes made by Mrs. Allingham.

1881.

GROUND FLOOR.

HALL.

Right-hand side.
Frederick Borck, Minister of King of Prussia.
Monmouth House (Smollett's), Lawrence Street, Chelsea.
Steele's House, Haverstock Hill, 1804.
Maurice, Comte de Lacy.
Pope.
Voltaire.

Left-hand side.
Warren Hastings.
John Forster's Library, Palace Gate.

FRONT DINING-ROOM.

East Wall.
Water-colour sketch by Mrs. Tom Taylor of Titian's " Charles V."
Steel engraving, "Cotter's Saturday Night."
Engravings of Frederick and Wilhelmina, Kosciusko, etc.
Count Pepoli.

FRONT DINING-ROOM—*continued.*

North Wall.

Water-colour by Count Pepoli.
Medallions of Goethe and John Sterling.
Medallions of Schiller and Edward Sterling ("The Thunderer").

West Wall.

Lady Ashburton.
A. Montague (ancestor of Lady Harriet Baring).
Antoin Graff.
Mr. Carlyle (lithograph from daguerrotype).
Leopold, Prince D'Anhalt Dessau.

South Wall.

Friedrich (engraving after Pesne).
Ferdinand of Brunswick.
Friedrich Wilhelm.
Cowper.

BACK DINING-ROOM.

North Wall.

David Hume.
Bismarck (photograph).
Friedrich.
Cromwell (medallion from bronze medal in possession of Colonel Nicholls).
Marquis of Argyll ("The Guid Marquis"), 1661.

West Wall—double doors.

Luther's portrait.

THE BACK DINING-ROOM (1881).

SOUTH WALL, WITH OLD SIDEBOARD AND WINE-COOLER, MRS. CARLYLE'S SCREEN, GOETHE'S PORTRAIT, ETC.

BACK DINING-ROOM—*continued.*

South Wall.

Maclise's sketch of Mr. Carlyle (" Fraser's Mag.").
Portrait of Goethe, 1825 (with Goethe's inscription
below).
Ziethen sitting before Friedrich (Chodowiecki).
Early portrait of Goethe (Wischer).
Lord Jeffrey.
Dante.

East Wall, over door.

Photograph of Sunnyside, Haddington.

SMALL ROOM.

West Wall.

Voltaire.
Rajon's etching of Watts' John Stuart Mill.
Maclise's sketch of Coleridge (" Fraser's Mag.").
Pencil sketch of Mrs. Carlyle by Miss Sketchley.
Cromwell's Wife.
Friedrich.
Lawrence's sketch of Mr. Carlyle.
Joseph II. of Austria.
Mrs. Carlyle (photograph by Mr. Tait).
Kate Sterling (chalk drawing by Anthony Sterling).

STAIRS.

Norborough, where died Elizabeth Cromwell, widow of
Oliver.
Francis I.
Maria Teresa.

STAIRS—*continued.*

Maupertuis.
Engel (Chodowiecki).
Landor.
Lessing.

FIRST FLOOR.

STAIRS.

Friedrich.　Oil-painting.
Friedrich, with Generals on horseback, after manœuvres
　　at Potsdam.
Goethe.

DRAWING-ROOM.

East Wall.

Sketch of Reims, by Edward Sterling.
Wilhelmina.
Cromwell (after Cooper).
Luther's Father (copied by Mr. R. Tait from portrait
　　at the Wartburg).
Luther's Mother (copied by Mr. R. Tait from portrait
　　at the Wartburg).

Door.

Frederick the Silent.　Albert Dürer.
Melancholia.　Albert Dürer.
Cromwell trampling on Scarlet Woman.
Cavaignac.
Sketch of Mr. Carlyle by Mrs. Allingham.
Anecdote Teatrale de l'homme unique à tout age.
Bearing the Cross.　Albert Dürer.

"THE LITTLE DRUMMER."
LARGE OIL PAINTING OF FRIEDRICH AND WILHELMINA, WHICH
HUNG ON SOUTH WALL OF DRAWING-ROOM.

DRAWING-ROOM—*continued.*

North Wall.

Miniature of Mrs. Carlyle as a girl, and photographs, candlesticks, etc.

West Wall.

Photographs of Ashburton family.
Miniature of Badams.
Three windows; mirrors between.

South Wall.

Portraits after photographs of Mr. and Mrs. Carlyle.
Large oil-painting, Friedrich and Wilhelmina with dog, after Pesne. (*See illustration.*)
Portrait of Mrs. Edward Sterling.
Portrait of Friedrich.

MRS. CARLYLE'S BEDROOM.

[*I have not been able to obtain any record of the wall decorations of this room during its occupancy by Mrs. Carlyle.*]

SECOND FLOOR.

STAIRS.

Shakespeare.
Mrs. Sterling.
Goethe's house at Weimar.

FRONT BEDROOM.

East Wall.
Monna Lisa.
Sophia Carolina (Friedrich's grandmother).
Chart.
Sophia Dorothea (Friedrich's mother).
Schiller; his Garden House; Goethe's House.
Thackeray Autographs.

North Wall.
Ziethen.
Canonicus Gleim.
Old Bible Woodcuts from John Sterling.

West Wall.
Voltaire (Caricatures).
Grandfather of Friedrich.
Elizabeth I. of Russia (" Catin du Nord ").
Friedrich.

South Wall.
Emerson.
Count Seckendorf.
Motley.
Sketch of Mr. Carlyle (by Count D'Orsay, May, 1839).
Thomas de Quincey.

MR. CARLYLE'S BEDROOM.

South Wall.
Maurice, Comte de Lacy.
" Friedrich on Parade; very good " (Chodowiecki).
Craigenputtock; two engravings.
" Oliver's Lord Broghil " (Broil); engraving.

DRAWINGS FROM CAST OF CARLYLE'S HEAD TAKEN AFTER DEATH.

X. Fourteen Years: 1881-1895.

THE history of No. 24, Cheyne Row, from 1881 to 1894,   Desolation.
may be briefly relegated to the "Great Empire of
Silence." After Carlyle's death there had been some
talk of an immediate purchase; but the contemplated arrangements fell through. Mr. and Mrs. Alexander Carlyle moved to
Wimbledon, and the house stood tenantless for several years. In   Carlyle's
1882 the beautiful bronze statue by Boehm was unveiled by   statue.
Professor Tyndall in the garden at the bottom of the Row, and a
little later a mural tablet (with a bas-relief of Carlyle) was affixed
on the wall at the south-eastern corner of the street, and was   Desecration.
afterwards, on the landlord's consent being obtained, re-fixed on
the front of No. 24. In 1887 (I think) a seven years' lease was
taken by a woman who had been living next door, and whose
tenancy became notorious by reason of the strange collection of
cats and dogs she accumulated here, which on several occasions
rendered police court proceedings necessary. By far too much was
made in the papers of this eccentric occupant and her belongings;
and I was struck in reading one of Mrs. Carlyle's earlier letters
to find that her addiction for bringing in lost animals, quadruped,

G

and biped, too, on occasion, once led her husband to suggest
that she should put a card in the window, " Home for strayed
cats and dogs." A climax was reached when the lady herself
succumbed, and a servant who continued in occupation intro-
duced inhabitants far more objectionable than Persian cats
and Maltese spaniels. However, in the summer of 1894 the
house was cleared and closed, and the wretched episode abruptly
ended.

Meanwhile, well meant but abortive attempts had been
made from various quarters, London and American, to rescue
and preserve the house. Ineffectual letters and protests appeared in the press from time to time, whilst private plans and
bargainings were equally barren of result, save that opinion was
tardily crystallizing in favour of some public effort to save the
place.

The purchase. The inception of the movement which has resulted in the
present Purchase was largely due to the efforts of Mr. George
Lumsden, of Heaton Chapel, to whom must be adjudged the final
honour of having, with infinite labour and tenacity of purpose,
coerced into concrete form and active energy the scattered forces
interested in this matter.

The record of the Purchase Fund is detailed elsewhere, and
here it need only be said that after active work had been begun
at Manchester, a timely impetus was given to the movement by
the offer of certain furnishings, books, etc., which came from
Mrs. Alexander Carlyle, who had been the companion of her
uncle's latest years, and had striven with unflagging energy in
vindication of his memory. A strong committee had been got
together before the headquarters of the fund were transferred to
the metropolis, where the first meeting was held in December ;
resulting in the appointment of Mr. Leslie Stephen as chairman,
the formation of an executive, and the arrangement of an active

canvass. Meanwhile, Chelsea had already expressed a desire to co-operate, and had sent an encouraging contribution in response to a local appeal.

The working body had no easy task. The moment (which was none of their choosing, being dictated by the expiry of the lease and threatened dilapidation) was not perhaps "psychological." The clouds of heated controversy and the dust of altercation raised by the publication of the "Memoirs," though thinned and broken, are not yet dispelled.

Here I may be allowed to quote part of a charming article in the "Speaker," the editor of which—almost alone among journalists—was a warm and active supporter of the Purchase Fund : Encouragement.

"The generation which knew Carlyle in the flesh when he was in his prime has disappeared, and even those who regarded him with a wistful sort of hero-worship in his closing years are rapidly diminishing in numbers. Froude's vivid and remarkable Life of the great man left a painful impression upon the minds of most of those who read it. It was too faithful a picture of an extraordinary life and character to be fully understood when it was first given to the world. So the generation which has derived its sole personal knowledge of Carlyle from his Memoirs is not by any means inclined to idealize him, or even to place him in his own true position as the greatest of the teachers of our century. . . . They do not know that, even at this moment, his influence, unseen and indirect though it may be, is among the most potent forces that are moving the mind of mankind.

"But we may very safely leave Thomas Carlyle's reputation to take care of itself. Few of us can have forgotten that magnificent outburst of heart-eloquence in which one of his dearest and most worthy friends compared the storm of detraction that raged round his head after the publication of the 'Memoirs,' to the gathering of a tempest round the Matterhorn. The winds blow and the clouds gather, and the air is made thick with the loathsome mist; and to the dwellers in the narrow vale among the hills it seems as though the mountain round whose brow the tempest rages had been blotted for ever from the skies. But far above the tumult of the storm the hoary crest of the Matterhorn stands in majestic peace, bathed in the radiance of the heavens. So, to Carlyle's friends and followers, it seems that it is with him, and, when the clouds have rolled away, he will be seen again in undimmed glory. When that day comes, and some future generation has grasped the secret of his greatness, men will wonder that in the year 1895 people begged in vain for the few pounds needed to preserve Carlyle's home to his countrymen for ever. It is not Carlyle alone, however, whose genius has made of the little house in Cheyne Row one of our national shrines. Even the dullards who now affect to despise him can hardly question the fact that during the greater portion of the Queen's reign he was the centre of the intellectual life of Britain. It was under his inspiration that poets, novelists, philosophers, politicians, and men of science worked. To him they came for the comfort that was to give them courage in the battle of life. From his lips they drew the words of counsel and of sympathy that armed them for the fight. It is, indeed, from their testimony that those who never met him in this life know best what he really was, and understand the heart of fire that beat beneath that form of granite. Thus it came to pass that, more than any other house in the land, the modest dwelling in Cheyne Row was, for a whole generation, the great gathering-place of English men of letters. A small house, truly; yet in it were born great thoughts that can never die, and within its rooms gathered great men whom posterity will well know how to reverence. It seems a mean and pitiful thing to have to beg for the small sum needed

THE GARRET STUDY (1857). SOUTH-EAST CORNER, WITH BOOKCASE, PORTRAITS AND MAPS FOR THE

to keep such a house amongst us as a national monument to not
the least of our national glories."

Apathy, disapproval, opposition, were freely encountered. All Opposition.
the fusty threadbare fallacies and heresies about the life at
Cheyne Row were dragged out once more, and stuck up as
scarecrows to warn off the unenlightened citizen whose guinea
might be captured unawares. Misconceptions, once vigorously
grafted, grow sturdily as weeds, and are as hard to eradicate ; and
it seems futile, even yet, for those who remember the realities, and
to whom the interior of " No. 5 " was a familiar vision and is a
delightful remembrance, to protest that the shadows of its por-
trayal have been so needlessly emphasized, and its brightness
and beauty so steadfastly ignored.

But dead horses may be excused flogging, and a word be ven- A catechism.
tured on the one fresh argument that was often raised in letters,
and was finally voiced in the columns of the " Manchester Guar-
dian " : " Are the Committee quite certain that Mr. Carlyle
would have in the very least degree sympathized with this well-
meant project of theirs ? " Into a region so speculative one
ventures with hesitation ; " quite certain," indeed, it would be
difficult under mortal circumstances to be ; and the more so that
the scriptures of Carlyle may sometimes be quoted to suit very
opposite purposes. But two points may be made towards the
conclusion that Carlyle, could he have regarded such a proposal
impersonally, would certainly not have disapproved it. First, he Hero-worship.
was essentially and consistently a hero-worshipper and a teacher
of hero-worship. " To give our approval aright, to do every one
of us what lies in him that the honourable man everywhere, and
he only have honour ; is not this the sum of all social morality ?
Imperfectly and not perfectly done, we know this duty must
always be. Not done at all, no longer remembered as a thing
which God and nature and the Eternal Voices do require to be

done—alas, we see too well what kind of a world that ultimately makes for us!" The whole argument of the "Hudson's Statue" pamphlet is not against memorials, but against the worship of false gods. *If* Hudson, *then* Cromwell would rather not, is its text. The essay seems to sum up the question of memorials plainly. To the worthy, the best that reverence and opportunity offer, imperfect though it be; to the unworthy, at no price any.

The other point affects the special question. If any, what? It is this. The first time Carlyle went abroad further than Paris, whither did he make his pilgrimage? To the homes of Luther, of Goethe, of Schiller. A few disjointed records are all that can be given : " Goethe's House ;—were in Goethe's room ; a little garret not much bigger than my dressing-room—and wrote our names in silence." " Eisenach with its Wartburg where Luther lay concealed translating the Bible ; there I spent one of the most interesting forenoons I ever got by travelling. . . . They open a door, you enter a little apartment, a very poor low room with an old leaden lattice window, to me the most venerable of all rooms I ever entered. . . . I kissed his old oak table, looked out of his window—making them open it for me—and thought to myself, ' Here once lived for a time one of God's soldiers. Be honour given him!'" This to his mother. To his wife he adds : " It was a real gain to me. I could not without worship look out of Luther's indubitable window, and reflect that here was authentically a kind of great man and a kind of holy place, if there were any such. . . . Goethe's house, which was opened by favour, kept us occupied in a strange mood for two hours and more, Schiller's for one. Goethe's house is quite like the picture, but . . . . small, low-roofed, and almost mean to what I had conceived ; hardly equal—nay, not at all equal, had my little architect once done her work—to my own at Chelsea. . . . Schiller's house was still more affecting; the room where he wrote, his old table, exactly like the model, the bed where he died, and a portrait of his dead face. A poor man's house, and a brave, who had fallen at his post there." " Unforgettable," he afterwards marked against these places of pilgrimage ; and how much of his account might not, *mutatis mutandis*, be written to-day of his own house here in Cheyne Row. " Here," he adds in a later description to Thomas Erskine, " tempted by the devil (always by ' devils' enough), but not subdued or subduable, stood God's truth, embodied in the usual way ; one man against all men ; it was there and in that way he dealt with the devil and defied him to his face. A scene worth visiting indeed." Carlyle, at least, found memorial houses intensely interesting and helpful ; and has recorded, with keenest appreciation, the visits he paid to the homes of Shakespeare, of Johnson, of Newton, of Smollett, of Burns, and others ; whilst pictures of the dwellings of Steele, of Elizabeth Cromwell, and of Sterling, as well as of those of Goethe, Schiller, and Smollett, hung on the walls of his own at Cheyne Row.

The canvass was pushed vigorously forward from the beginning of 1895. Circulars and letters were widely distributed, the assistance of libraries throughout the country was invoked, and, by the invitation of the Lord Mayor, a crowded meeting was held at the Mansion House at the end of February, and addressed by Lord Ripon, the United States Ambassador, Mr. Leonard Courtney, Mr. Leslie Stephen, and Mr. Crockett. Funds came in slowly but steadily ; auxiliary committees were formed in New York and in Glasgow, and over £400 was remitted from America. By the end of April about £2,000 had been collected, sufficient to complete the purchase, pay the expenses of the fund, and carry out part of the essential repairs. The freehold of the house was accordingly bought in May, and, after a careful survey of its

Collection of funds.

actual condition, the necessary works were put in hand at the
end of the month, and completed in June.

The end of the season in London, and the occurrence of a
General Election in July, rendered the arrangement of any
opening ceremony impossible, and the House was therefore
opened informally at the end of July, and was visited by over a
thousand persons, from all parts of the world, during the next
six weeks.

We do not now call our great men Gods
nor admire without limit; ah no,
with limit enough! But if
we have no great men, or
do not admire at all,
—that were a
still worse
case.

Mr. Carlyle's Bedroom—*continued.*

South Wall.

Two lithographs of John Sterling (one, " bad likeness,"
the other, " liker, not like ").

Graf v. Bruhl (" 365 suits in the year ").

Robespierre haranguing the crowd (oil-painting by
Mrs. Paulet).

Friedrich Wilhelm (engraving).

" Il Segretario Ambulante " (coloured print).

Sir John Hawkins " without his shoes and stockings."

Victor Cousin, James Watt, Immanuel Kant (photographs).

Col. Gardiner (of Preston Pans) ; engraving.

Henricus Princeps Borussiæ.

Spinosa.

Samuel Graf von Schmettau (engraving).

East Wall.

Friedrich II.   Old mirror beneath.

Photograph of the Arched House, Ecclefechan, where
Mr. Carlyle was born.

North Wall.

Mr. Carlyle's old desk with drawers.

Photograph of the Abbey Church at Haddington, and
Mrs. Carlyle's grave.

Large oil portrait of Mr. Carlyle's mother.

West Wall.

Portraits : Seidlitz, Friedrich II., Winterfeld.

Friedrich II. examining a school.

SMALL DRESSING-ROOM.

Lord Bacon.
Sphinx in the Desert (photograph).
Sterling's house at Jamaica (coloured engraving).

South Wall.

Shelf, clothes pegs, small round mirror.

East Wall.

John Sterling's grave, Bonchurch (photograph).
Emerson (photograph).
Dressing-table.
Goethe, Schiller, Bismarck.

North Wall.

Edward Irving.
House at Nürnberg where Schiller's mother was born.
Lord Marlborough (John Churchill).
Group of photographs of Mrs. Carlyle.

West Wall.

Small fireplace, over:
Bronze statuette of Napoleon.
Thomas Erskine of Linlathen.
Group of family photographs.

Over door:
Engravings of Jean Paul and Klopstock.

Nature admits
no lie.

NOTES TO THE PLANS.

Garret Floor Plan.

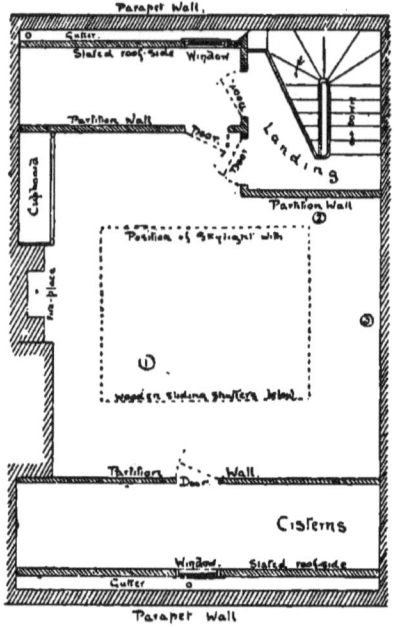

1 Writing Table   2 Double bookcase   3 Couch

The walls were hung with maps, engravings and portraits of Friedrich

It is here then that the spiritual majority of Teufelsdröckh commences. He has discovered that the Ideal workshop he so panted for is even this same Actual ill-furnished workshop he has so long been stumbling in.

THE GARRET ROOM.

THE arrangement of this room, which was built in 1853, occupied by Carlyle till 1865, and afterwards used as a servant's bedroom, is clearly indicated on the plan; whilst Mr. Tait's photographs (taken in 1857) give an excellent record of its aspect. Indeed, it is not often that so famous a literary workshop has been so faithfully depicted for posterity. The spacious skylight which drove Carlyle to despair by besmutting his books and papers, gave his visitor the abundant light which indoor photography so often lacks, and the result is a series of pictures of wonderful interest. Mr. Tait was good enough to entrust the negatives to me to make my own prints; and it was, indeed, a fascinating employment to resuscitate, by a few minutes of exposure to light, these speaking records of the dead past of nearly forty years ago. By their aid we have little difficulty in mentally reconstituting the "soundless room" as it was during Carlyle's "thirteen years' war" there. Entering by the door at the head of the staircase (a second door opens into the cupboard space, though for what reason, unless to provide a means of escape, is not obvious) one finds immediately to one's right hand a third door into this same closet. Beyond it, against the partition wall, stood a half-round table with an oilcloth cover, carrying books and papers; above it hung a small portrait of Carlyle's mother, an engraving of Frederick on horseback, and a map, pinned on the wall, unframed. On the north wall, to the right of the fireplace, shelved cupboards were fitted. Over the square white marble mantelpiece, with its "merely human" fireplace and white-tiled sides, hung several small sketches and engravings around the wooden pulley board, to which were attached the lines for the sliding shutter and the ventilators. On the left of the fire, above a circular silk-pleated screen, hung a paper rack and some written notes on Friedrich, probably chronological. On the mantel stood two white china candlesticks, and a small bronze statuette of Napoleon. In the further corner, to the left of the fireplace, was a high upright cabinet with drawers for manuscripts, prints, etc.; and on the western wall there were bookshelves to right and left of the door leading into the closet behind the partition.

Against the southern wall stood a low couch with loose leather mattress; while the eastern side, from the corner to the door, was occupied by a long, dwarf, three-tiered bookshelf, the upper half of which was filled with the works of Voltaire, in over ninety volumes. Maps, prints, and engravings, relating almost exclusively to the "Life of Frederick the Great," covered the available wall space; and in one corner stood the long, hooked pole by which the balanced frames of the skylight could be opened and closed. Near the fireplace, a little to the left, was the place of the famous writing-table on which so much of noble work had painful birth. The photograph gives so exact an impression of its sturdy frame, its broad folding flap, its slightly boxed top, and back drawers, that no further description is needed either of it or the solid writing-chair. Hard by stood another little table on castors, which carried the books in immediate use (or

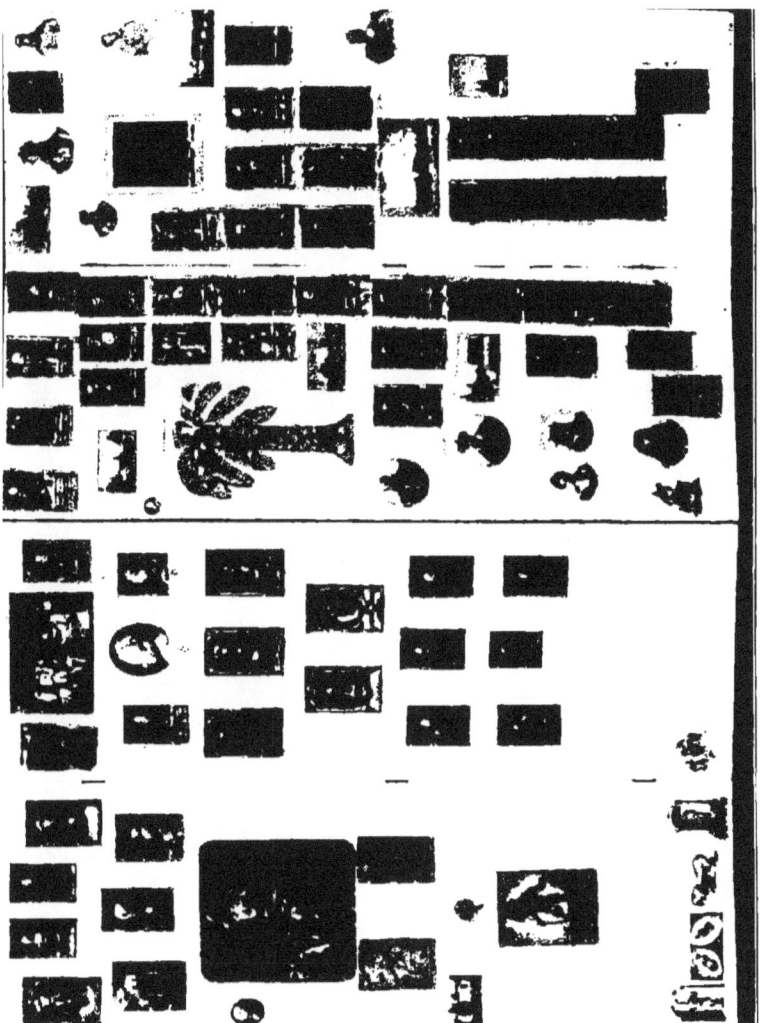

THE PORTRAIT SCREEN IN THE GARRET STUDY (1857).

such as were not on the floor !), while behind was the fourfold screen on which were pasted near a hundred old portrait prints, to which the maker of history always turned for insight and guidance in depicting his characters.

All readers of Carlyle will remember how greatly he depended on these presentments for insight and guidance in depicting his characters.

" Every student and reader of History," he wrote, " who strives earnestly to conceive for himself what manner of Fact and *Man* this or the other vague Historical *Name* can have been, will, as the first and directest indication of all, search eagerly for a Portrait, for all the reasonable Portraits there are ; and never rest till he have made out, if possible, what the Man's natural face was like.   Often I have found a portrait superior in real instruction to half-a-dozen written ' Biographies,' as Biographies are written ; or rather let me say, I have found that the Portrait was as a small lighted *candle* by which the Biographies could for the first time be read, and some human interpretation made of them."

When Carlyle gave up the use of this room, after the completion of his great history, the pictures, books, and furniture were dispersed elsewhere about the house, and later visitors will remember the writing-desk as standing in the drawing-room, the cabinet of drawers and little table in the dining-room, and many of the prints in the hall, staircase, and elsewhere, as indicated in the Picture List appended.

His Book, as indeed most good Books
are, has been written, in many
senses, with his heart's
blood.

Second Floor Plan.

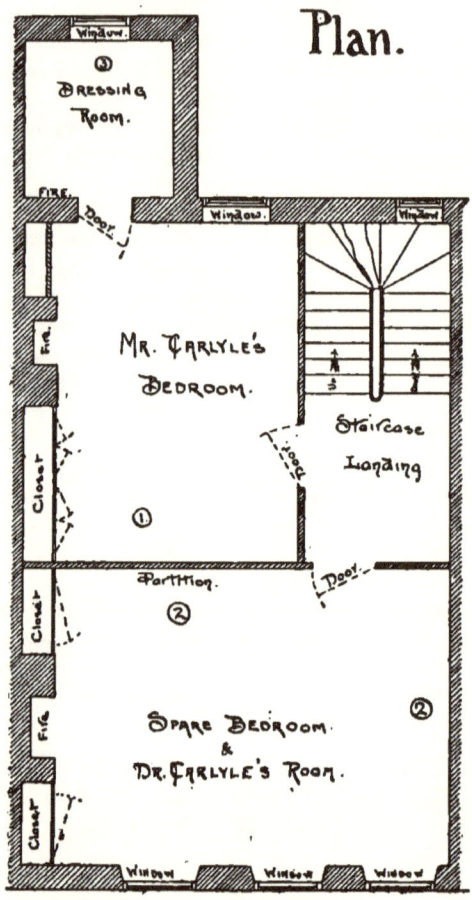

1. Carlyle's bed. 2. Bed.
3. Dressing Table. (Emerson slept here).

> Effect? Influence? Utility? Let a man do his work; the fruit of it is the care of Another than he.～～～～～～

THE SECOND FLOOR.

The Spare Bedroom.—This is a pretty, bright, three-windowed room, with partly panelled walls, and a beautiful little fireplace. The bed stood with its head against the southern wall. Amongst the pictures were portraits of Friedrich's grandmother and mother, of Motley, of De Quincey, and of Emerson ; sketches of Schiller's and Goethe's homes ; Voltaire caricatures ; autographs of Thackeray ; and the drawing of Carlyle caught by Count D'Orsay—I think surreptitiously—during one of his visits.

Mr. Carlyle's Bedroom.—The fine old wooden four-post curtained bed stands in its old place against the western wall, and behind it is the long fixed wardrobe of grained painted wood. The bold broad sash mouldings of the window, with its half panes at the top; the nice old grate ; and the unpanelled over-mantel on which was probably (as elsewhere in the Row) a raised framed picture panel at one time, will be noticed here. The styles of the wainscoting were painted, and the panels papered and covered with pictures, of which a very interesting list is given elsewhere. Over the fireplace hung the large full-face oil portrait of Carlyle's mother, and on the mantelshelf always lay the Bible (in 2 vols.) given by his mother on his leaving home for College ; whilst drawings and photographs

K

of his Ecclefechan birthplace, of Craigenputtock, of the Abbey Church at Haddington, and of members of his and his wife's families, filled other places on the walls. The little dressing-room beyond, too, was well filled with pictures, except the south wall, which was occupied by a shelf, a row of coat pegs, and a small looking-glass. The small dressing-table stood by the window, and close about it hung pictures of friends and heroes, of Goethe and Schiller, of Emerson and Irving, of Neuberg, the untiring companion of many tours, of Erskine, the honoured "St. Thomas" of Linlathen, and of John Sterling's house and grave. Over the tiny fireplace, which Carlyle had added, stood —after the garret room was given up—the little statuette of Napoleon, of whom he had contemplated, and abandoned, the thought of a biography.

It is the Noblest, not the Sham Noblest; it is God Almighty's Noble, not the Court Cailor's Noble, nor the Able Editor's Noble, that must in some approximate degree be raised to the supreme place; he and not a counterfeit, — under penalties!

First Floor Plan.

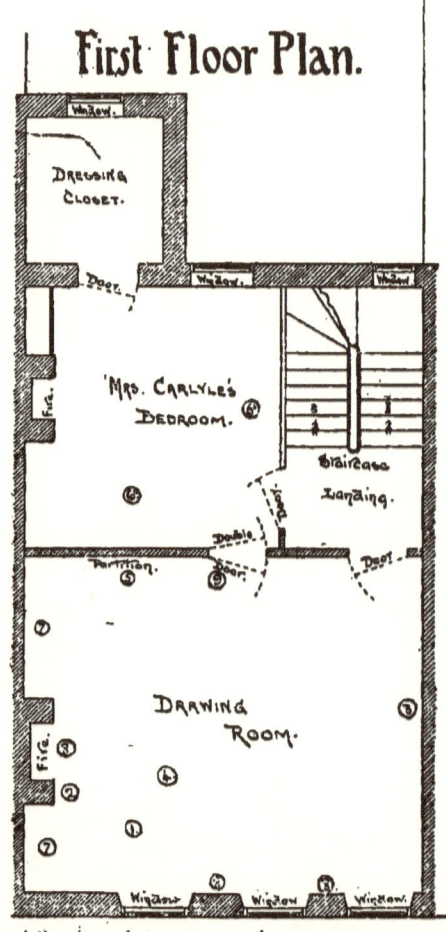

1. MRS. CARLYLE'S SOFA.   4. WORK TABLE.
2. MR. CARLYLE'S FLOOR SEAT. 5. PIANO.
3. LARGE PICTURE.   6. FOUR POST BED.
   (FRIEDRICH & WILHELMINA.)   (TWO POSITIONS.)
        7. BOOKCASE WITH CUPBOARDS BELOW.
8. MIRRORS. 9. MR CARLYLE'S WRITING DESK (LATTERLY)

> **Man is perennially interesting to man; nay, if we look strictly to it, there is nothing else interesting.**

THE FIRST FLOOR.

The Drawing-Room.—There are happily many yet left amongst us to whom the memories of this pleasant room during Mrs. Carlyle's lifetime are still freshly delightful. The white window blinds admitted ample, yet subdued, light; the large mirror over the mantelshelf, given by Lord (or Lady) Ashburton, reflected a pretty vista of the three curtained windows, or repeated the children's faces in the large picture of " The Little Drummer" which occupied the southern wall; the bookcases, with cup-boards below, which filled the recesses to right and left of the fire, lent character and warmth of tone. The massive steel Bramah grate, with its panelled hob sides, and blue and white figured Dutch tiles; the long red, double-ended sofa by the window which Mrs. Carlyle used so much; the big green leather armchair (presented by John Forster) with its sockets and swivel writing-desk, which was Carlyle's usual seat in later years; the oval table, with the large china inkstand, the elephant letter weight, and Dickens' " boy on the gate;" the black fleece hearthrug; the pierced brass fender; the little cottage piano, with its shiny, turned legs; the double door opening into Mrs. Carlyle's bedroom; the portraits of Cromwell, of Wilhelmina, and of Luther's parents; the Dürer drawings; these, and a dozen other details, dwell yet in living memories.

Mrs. Carlyle's Bedroom.—Our records of this room are, of course, less exact. The large four-post bed, to which allusion has already been made, stood between the door and the window ; and we recall Carlyle's reference to some ingenious rope mechanism which she contrived for lifting and moving herself in bed when disabled by her illness. Her letters contain many references to its arrangements, changes of furniture, re-papering, pictures and photographs.

After 1866 it was occupied by Carlyle's niece, Miss Aitken (afterwards Mrs. Alexander Carlyle) ; and Carlyle himself was moved down here before his last illness.[1]

[1] Carlyle was moved down into this room late in November or early in December, 1880, about a month before his last illness, because of its nearness to the drawing-room (where he nearly always sat), thus saving him the effort of climbing the stairs, which, owing to his increasing weakness, was growing more and more trying. During the unusually cold weather of January following, some three weeks before his death, a bed was put up in the drawing-room at Dr. M'Clagan's suggestion, and he was moved in there, it being the largest and warmest room in the house.

What hast thou done, and how ? Happiness, unhappiness; all that was but the wages thou hadst.

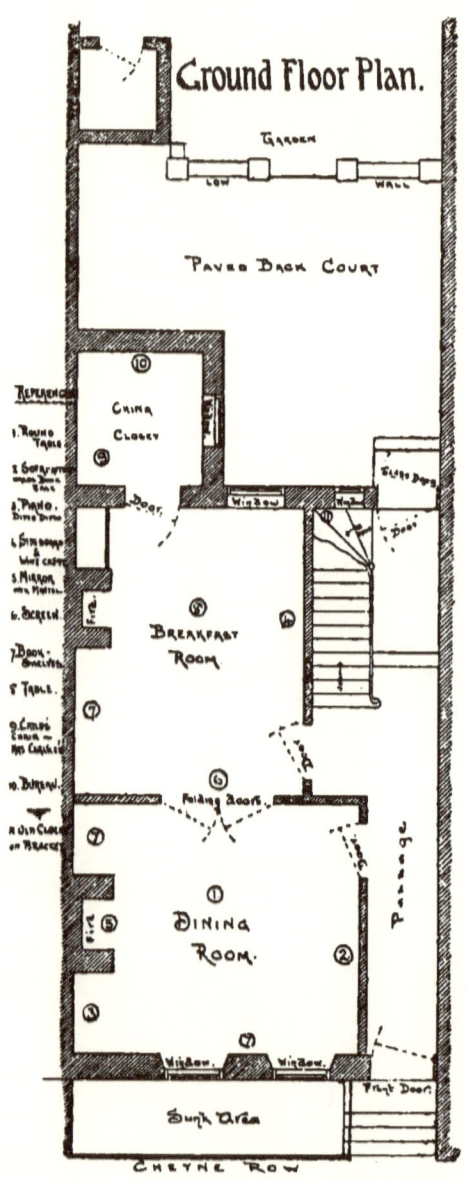

Ground Floor Plan.

GARDEN

LOW WALL

PAVED BACK COURT

REFERENCES

1. ROUND TABLE
2. SOFA WITH PILLOW
3. PIANO DITTO DITTO
4. SIDEBOARD & WINE CHEST
5. MIRROR OVER MANTEL
6. SCREEN
7. BOOK SHELVES
8. TABLE
9. CARLYLE'S CHAIR OR MRS CARLYLE'S
10. BUREAU
11. OLD CLOCK ON BRACKET

CHINA CLOSET

Window

Door

BREAKFAST ROOM

Fire

Folding Doors

DINING ROOM.

Fire

Window   Window

Passage

Front Door

SUNK AREA

CHEYNE ROW

To this hour no public matter, with whatever serious argument, can be settled in England, till it have been dined upon, perhaps repeatedly dined upon.~~~~

THE GROUND FLOOR.

The Dining-Room.—Of the look and arrangement of these ground floor rooms, in the fifties, we have a very accurate and detailed record in Mr. Tait's picture " An Interior at Chelsea." The double doors between the front and back rooms were kept open,[1] forming one long chamber. The floor was carpeted throughout, and the upper walls papered on canvas stretched over the fine old panelled wainscoting ; both being figured with a large pattern. The front dining-room fireplace was similar to the one in the drawing-room above, except that the tiles were larger and of cream colour with brown designs. Excellently planned bookcases, with cupboards and drawers below, filled the recesses on either side of the fireplace as well as that opposite the door in the back room ; whilst the large set of shelves, when brought down from the drawing-room, occupied the wall facing the fireplace in the front room. Quaint little episodes are re-called as one stands by this plain square marble mantel. It was at this spacious grate that Mrs. Carlyle—the kitchen fire having failed in briskness at a critical moment—was completing

---

[1] The large bookcase closed up the door from the passage into the front room.

L

one of her famous brews of marmalade, " pure as liquid amber "
(her recipe is cherished still at my home) when a loud knock at
the front door close by, announced Southey's first visit. One
remembers, too, that other fireplace—his mother's at Scotsbrig
—where the number of the "Athenæum " containing a vehement
castigation of " The French Revolution"—sent in by a too
friendly neighbour—was found to have been pressed into un-
willing service to boil a lagging breakfast-kettle. An eight-legged
round table in two parts occupied the centre of this front room ;
a small sofa stood between the windows ;[1] an upright cabinet
filled the corner nearest the front door; pictures, here as everywhere, were numerous, so that but little of the walls was
visible. A set of solidly-built dining-room chairs of mahogany
and horse-hair, and a handsome old brass fender and copper coal-
box completed the essential furnishings of this room. Cane
blinds shielded the lower window panes from inquisitive passers-
by, and Venetians hung above.

Of *the Back Dining-Room* the principal piece of furniture was
a large antique sideboard with rounded corner swing drawers,
beneath which stood an octagonal " wine cooler." Near—sometimes across—the double doorway was the large screen which
Mrs. Carlyle had covered with hundreds of pictorial cuttings.
Here too stood in early years the cage of Chico the songster ;
and the little armchair which had been Mrs. Carlyle's when
a child. " Her little bit of a first chair, its wee, wee arms : I
have looked at it hundreds of times, from of old, with many
thoughts." From the window one gets a pleasant glimpse across
the flagged court and down the little bush-grown garden, with
its step and parapet and old buttressed, creeper-clad side wall.

---

[1] There were also bookshelves (fitted or fixed) between the front windows,
and between the back window and china closet door, extending from about
three feet from the floor to the cornice.

DINING-ROOM. NORTH WALL AND FIREPLACE (1881).

In the small third room, or china closet, opening out at the back, stood a pretty old bureau, while the walls carried a miscellaneous group of portraits—Voltaire and John Stuart Mill, Coleridge and Cromwell's wife, Joseph II. of Austria and Mrs. Carlyle. Amongst many interesting pictures in these rooms three may be specially mentioned: the engraving of Ziethen sitting before Frederick, which hung over the sideboard; the portrait of Luther, on the west wall to the left of the folding doors; and the portrait of Goethe (also over the sideboard, above the disputed John Knox), beneath which Goethe himself had written the lines:

> "Liegt dir Gestern klar und offen,
> Wirkst du Heute kräftig frey
> Kannst auch auf ein Morgen hoffen
> Das nicht minder glücklich sey.
>   GOETHE."

Weimar. 7 *Nov.*
1825.

Wise command, wise obedience; the capability of these two is the net measure of culture and human virtue in every man.

Basement Plan.

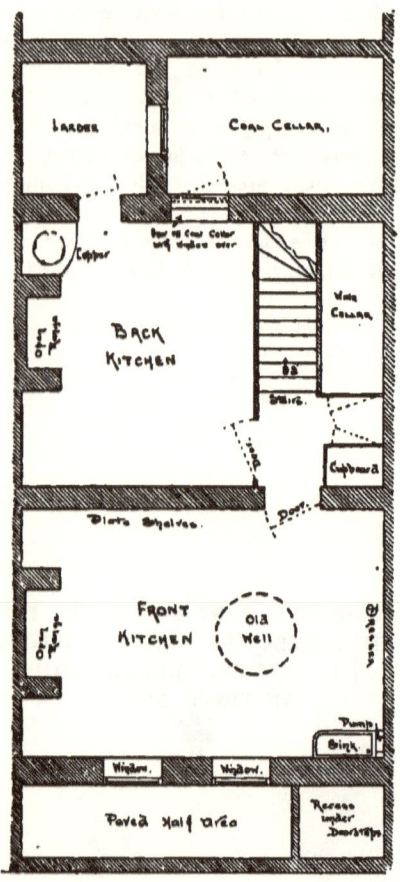

> ℭf a truth, if man were not a poor hungry bastard, and even much of a blockhead withal, he would cease criticising his victuals to such extent; and criticise himself rather, what he does with his victuals!

THE BASEMENT.

To readers of the " Letters and Memorials," many glimpses of this kitchen floor and its occupants will occur. It was not, indeed, quite an ideal place of service ; somewhat dark in winter, stone-flagged, and apt to be damp, the outer area not having been (till recently) sunk below the level of the windows. The old open kitchener with its broad bars, its kettle-crane, and its screw adjustment for the fire space, makes one regret the victorious incursion of close ranges ; while the disconnected pump recalls the days when the best of water might safely be drawn from the Chelsea gravel.

Shall I tell you which is the one intolerable sort of slavery; the slavery ober which the bery Gods weep? It is the slavery of the strong to the weak; of the great and nobleminded to the small and mean! The slavery of Wisdom to Folly.

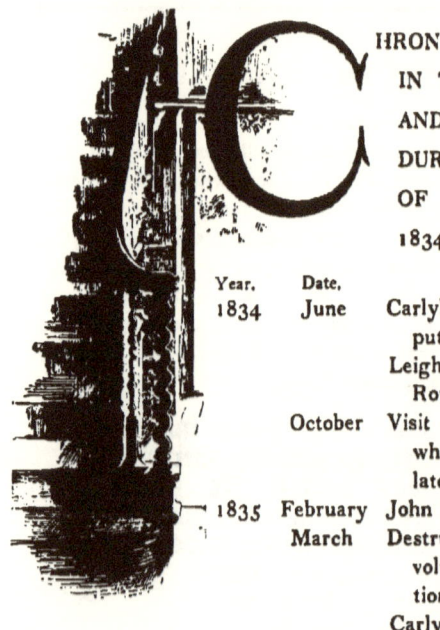

HRONOLOGY OF EVENTS
IN THE LIVES OF MR.
AND MRS. CARLYLE
DURING THEIR TENANCY
OF 5, CHEYNE ROW.
1834—1881.

Year.	Date.	Event.
1834	June	Carlyle's move from Craigenputtock to 5, Cheyne Row. Leigh Hunt often at Cheyne Row.
	October	Visit from Edward Irving, who died two months later.
1835	February	John Mill at Cheyne Row.
	March	Destruction of MS. of first volume of " French Revolution." Carlyle meets Southey and Wordsworth.
	September	First volume " French Revolution " re-written.

Year.	Date.	Event.
1836	April	"Sartor Resartus" published in America.
	May	John Sterling much at Cheyne Row.
		"Diamond Necklace" published in "Fraser."
1837	Jan. 12	"French Revolution" finished.
		Miss Martineau visits Carlyle.
	May 1	First course of Lectures at Willis's Rooms, "German Literature."
	June 1	"French Revolution" published.
1838	May	Second course of Lectures, "Periods of European Culture."
		Carlyle meets F. Maurice and Thomas Erskine.
1839	January	Carlyle meets Bunsen, Hallam, and Pusey at Monckton Milnes'; also Mr. Baring, afterwards Lord Ashburton. London Library founded at Carlyle's instigation. "Sartor Resartus" published in book form in England.
	February	Mrs. Carlyle's only "Soirée."
	April	Count D'Orsay at Cheyne Row.
	May	Third course of Lectures, "Revolutions of Modern Europe."
		Mr. Marshall gives Carlyle a horse, "Citoyenne."
	December	"Chartism" published.
1840	May	Fourth course of Lectures, "Hero-Worship."
		Thirlwall visits Carlyle.
	June	Articles on Carlyle in the "Edinburgh" and "Quarterly" Reviews.

Year.	Date.	Event.
1840	July	Tennyson at Cheyne Row.
		Carlyle at work on " Cromwell."
1841		" Hero-Worship" published.
	February	Carlyle serves on a special jury.
		Carlyle invited to stand for the Chair of History at Edinburgh.
1842	February	Death of Mrs. Carlyle's mother.
	May	Carlyle visits Dr. Arnold at Rugby.
	August	Carlyle at Bruges and Ghent.
		Owen, the Naturalist, visits Carlyle.
	September	Carlyle rides through Cromwell's country.
1843	April	" Past and Present" published.
	July	Carlyle visits Wales and Scotland.
		Repairs and paint at Cheyne Row.
	November	Carlyle " over head and ears in ' Cromwell.' "
1844		Carlyle visits Mr. and Lady Harriet Baring at Addiscombe.
	September 18	Death of Sterling.
1845	August	John Forster at Cheyne Row.
	December	" Cromwell " published.
1846	June	Correspondence with Sir Robert Peel on " Cromwell."
	September	Carlyle in Ireland; hears O'Connell's last speech at Conciliation Hall, Dublin.
1847	May	Jeffrey and Dr. Chalmers at Cheyne Row.
	August	Carlyle visits W. E. Forster at Rawdon.
	September	Carlyle meets John and Jacob Bright at Rochdale.
		Emerson visits England.
1848	March	Carlyle meets Macaulay and Sir R. Peel.

Year.	Date.	Event.
1848	April 10	The Chartist Petition.
	July	Emerson and Carlyle visit Stonehenge together.
		Death of Charles Buller.
	April	Louis Blanc at Cheyne Row.
1849	May	Mazzini "one of the three kings of Rome."
	June	Froude's first visit to Cheyne Row.
		Carlyle visits Ireland.
	December	Paper on the Negro Question. Carlyle severs connection with Mill. Arrival of "Nero."
1850	January-July	"Latter-Day Pamphlets."
	May and June	Carlyle dines with Sir Robert Peel, and meets the Duke of Wellington at Bath House.
	July	Carlyle visits Savage Landor at Bath.
1851	January	The original of "Blanche Amory" staying at Cheyne Row.
		Carlyle's visit to Pentonville Jail.
	May	"Life of John Sterling." The Industrial Exhibition.
1852	January	Carlyle begins his "Life of Frederick the Great."
	July	Visit to Fife and Germany. Repairs at Cheyne Row, lasting till November.
	September	Carlyle visits the houses of Goethe, Schiller, and Luther.
	October	Thieves at Cheyne Row in Carlyle's absence.
		Occasional discourse on the Nigger Question.

M

Year.	Date.	Event.
1853	July	Building of the sound-proof room begun.
	December	Death of Carlyle's mother; he with her at Scotsbrig.
1854		Carlyle at work on "Frederick" in the new garret room.
		Geraldine Jewsbury came to live in Chelsea.
1855	November	Mrs. Carlyle conducts an appeal before the Income Tax Commissioners.
1856	August	Carlyles in Scotland; Edinburgh, Haddington, the Gill, and Scotsbrig.
1857	May	Death of Lady Ashburton.
	August	Mrs. Carlyle's health failing. In Scotland again.
	August	Second tour in Germany. Visits to Frederick's battle-fields.
1858	September	First volumes of "Frederick" published.
	December	Lord Ashburton's second marriage.
1859	June	Carlyle takes a house at Humbie in Fife. Mrs. Carlyle's ill-health increases.
1860	February	"Nero" died.
	August	Carlyle to Aberdeen and Thurso.
1861	April	Carlyle to hear Ruskin's Lecture on "Leaves."
1862	August	Carlyle writes to Erskine eulogising Ruskin's "Unto this last."
1863	February	Carlyle's horse "Fritz" comes down with him, and is sold.
	April	Carlyle goes to one of Dickens' Readings.
	August	Mrs. Carlyle falls in St. Martin's Lane and sprains her thigh.

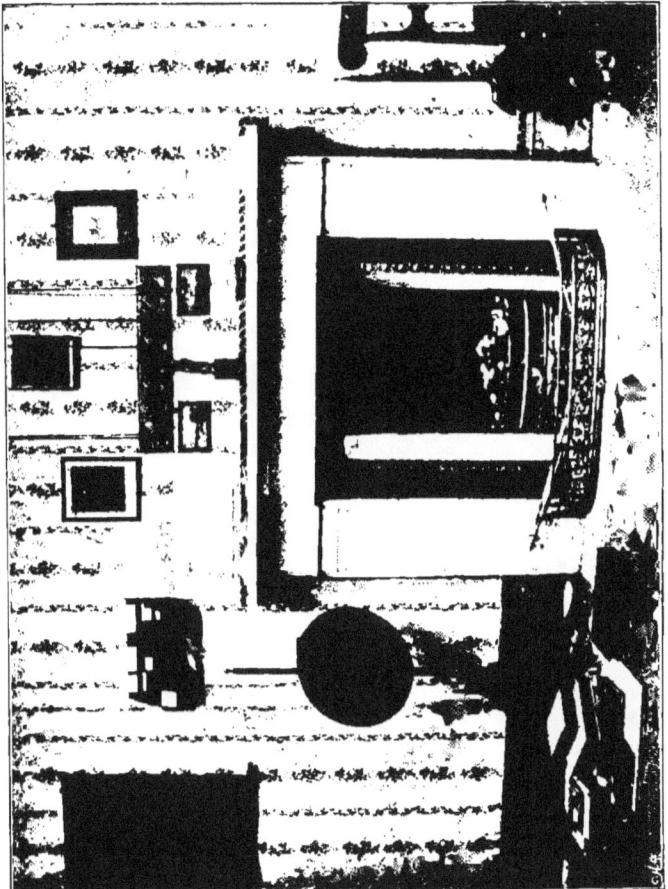

THE GARRET STUDY (1857). FIREPLACE AND NORTH WALL.

Year.	Date.	Event.
1864	March	Mrs. Carlyle's illness grows worse. She is taken to St. Leonards, thence to Scotland.
	October	Mrs. Carlyle returns to Cheyne Row, "weak, shattered, body worn to a shadow, spirit bright as ever." Carlyle buys his wife a brougham.
1865	April	Last volume of "Frederick" published. Carlyles to Devonshire, with Lady Ashburton.
	November	Elected Lord Rector of University of Edinburgh.
1866	April 2	Inaugural Address at Edinburgh. Professor Tyndall accompanies Carlyle.
	Sat. „ 21	Sudden death of Mrs. Carlyle.
	23	Carlyle arrives from Dumfries at Cheyne Row.
	26	Mrs. Carlyle buried in the nave of the old Abbey Kirk at Haddington.
	April	Message of condolence from the Queen.
	June	John Carlyle comes to Cheyne Row.
1867	January	Carlyle at Mentone. Meets Gladstone.
	June	Carlyle bequeaths Craigenputtock to Edinburgh University.
	August	"Shooting Niagara" published.
	November	Carlyle goes a little pilgrimage to Woolsthorpe, Sir Isaac Newton's birthplace.
1868	January	Carlyle to Tyndall's Lecture on Faraday.
	October	Carlyle again thrown, riding "Comet."
1869	January	Carlyle meets the Queen at Westminster Deanery.

Year.	Date.	Event.
1869	April	Carlyle at work editing his wife's letters.
1870	March	Death of Mr. Erskine, of Linlathen.
	November	Carlyle writes to the " Times " on Franco-Prussian War.
1871	March	Carlyle loses use of his right hand.
	June	Carlyle takes Froude the " Letters and Memorials," and " Reminiscences."
1872	February	The " Norse Kings " finished.
	November	Emerson in England.
1873	May	Death of Mill.
1874	February	Carlyle receives the Prussian Order of Merit.
	December	Disraeli offers Carlyle the Grand Cross of the Bath.
1875		" Early Kings of Norway." " Portraits of John Knox."
	December 4	Carlyle's eightieth birthday. " A whirlwind of gifts and congratulations."
1876	February	Death of John Forster.
	April	Carlyle's brother Alick died.
1877	May	Letter to the " Times " on Russo-Turkish War.
		Carlyle's statue executed by Boehm, and portrait by Millais.
1878		Carlyle's weakness steadily increasing.
1879		Death of John Carlyle.
1880	October	Carlyle growing weaker and in doctor's hands.
1881	February 5	Carlyle's death.
	„ 10	Carlyle buried at Ecclefechan.

> How could the Philosophy of Clothes, and the Author of such Philosophy, be brought home, in any measure, to the business and bosoms of our own English Nation?

NOTES TO THE ILLUSTRATIONS.

Frontispiece. (Thomas Carlyle, 1854.)

REFERENCE to this portrait, and Carlyle's appreciation of it, is made in the prefatory note. The negative was broken in two (fortunately, not across the face), and the film chipped and damaged ; but a satisfactory impression was nevertheless obtainable.

Dedication Page.

This profile of Carlyle has been carefully drawn from a small relief rapidly worked by the late Sir Edgar Boehm in brown wax on a tile, now in my possession. The strength and vigour of this rough little impression from life are remarkable.

Maps of Old and Modern Chelsea.

I hope that these plans of the Chelsea of two centuries ago and of to-day may interest visitors to this famous old quarter, and may serve as a guide to some of the notable houses in its earlier and later history. The first map has been drawn for this work from Hamilton's survey of 1664 (which is included in Faulkner's "History of Chelsea"), and has been corrected by me in certain details from a series of manuscript plans drawn by

Dr. King, who was Rector of the parish during the last decade of the seventeenth century, and left various valuable records of his cure here.   On the second map (in which, for clearness, many smaller streets have been omitted) an index of the houses of interest during the last two centuries has been incorporated.

The Ground Floor Rooms : " An Interior at Chelsea."

This block is reproduced from a pen-and-ink drawing of Mr. Tait's picture, which was painted by him in 1857, from a low seat in the south-west window of the dining-room at 5, Cheyne Row. The perspective was much criticised at the time, and no doubt the point of view gives an impression of somewhat greater length than actually exists.   But this does not affect the value of so detailed and interesting a record, which was fully recognized when the picture was exhibited.

The sketches of the

Drawing-room,

from Mr. Baly's photographs, will revive familiar memories for some who spent unforgettable hours there.   They were taken in 1881, the year of Carlyle's death ; but the arrangements of the room had only been very slightly altered—the door opening into Mrs. Carlyle's bedroom being closed and curtained—since her lifetime.

View Eastward from the House.

This photograph reveals the changes which forty years have brought to the neighbourhood of Cheyne Row, and helps us to realize the " mere leafy greenness " upon which in earlier years its back windows looked, before Oakley Street flats and houses, steam laundries, model dwellings, and Roman Catholic churches had arisen to mar the peaceful prospects of the quiet little terrace. The photograph shows the arrangement of the white awning which was rigged, with so much labour, in summer; and the two curious china seats, often referred to in Mrs. Carlyle's letters; and Carlyle's heelless slippers are typical of the easy *negligee* for which he appreciated his garden.

Portrait of Mrs. Carlyle. 1855.

Mr. Tait's photographs of Mr. and Mrs. Carlyle were taken at the back of his house in Queen Anne Street. He found Mrs. Carlyle a more difficult subject than her husband. She was prone to that camera self-consciousness which is the photographer's worst enemy. She liked to have warning of the removal of the cap, and the result was generally a set expression about the eyes and lips. But Mr. Tait contrived to take this photograph *without* the warning, and obtained a natural, unconstrained and characteristic likeness. This negative was also unfortunately cracked and damaged, though not very seriously.

The little sketch of the charming old

Fireplace in the Guest-Chamber

has additional interest as having been kindly drawn for me by a grand-niece of Thomas Carlyle.

The reproductions of Mr. Tait's photographs of the

Garret Study

give an exact and faithful record of a famous room. The plate on which Carlyle was taken at work at his writing-desk was unluckily deficient in silver, and the negative consequently lacks detail; but the subject was so interesting that I could not resist including it in the series. The writing hand is unfortunately indefinite, but the position of the feet and left hand are characteristic; on the table, with papers, gum-bottle, seal, etc., is the curious screw ink-well, which has now been replaced in the house. Much of the features of the portraits on the Friedrich Screen is also inevitably lost in the photo-etching.

The Letter from Thomas Carlyle to Allan Cunningham

("Honest Allan," the Dumfriesshire mason-poet), reproduced in facsimile, was written from the lodging in Ampton Street, at which he resided on several occasions before the move to Chelsea. The "scriptory ware" no doubt refers to "Sartor Resartus," which was just then going the hopeless round of London publishers, and had been returned by one of the most eminent of them with the encouraging dictum "that the writer only required a little more tact to produce a popular as well as an able work." Happy, indeed, was it that Teufelsdröckh's biographer was not of the stuff that could be crushed by the contemptuous "Testimony of the High-Class Bookseller's Taster," and could, as here, answer the Everlasting No with Homeric laughter, and "A fig for thee, Nicholas!"

The Letter from Mrs. Carlyle to Mr. Tait

is one of two which were kindly lent me for reproduction by him. The one which appears in facsimile is a very charming and characteristic specimen of her style. I give it here, as the writing is perhaps less absolutely legible than her husband's:

SUNNY BANK,
HADDINGTON.
[*Mr. Tait has added the date, August 12th,* 1856.]

MY DEAR MR. TAIT,

I do think you are the kindest man alive! Thank you with all my heart for the beautiful little photographs—If you only knew how they are valued here! [These were copies from

6. Woburn Buildings, Tavistock Square
Tuesday.

My Dear Cunningham,

I will with very great pleasure come over on Saturday, as you invite: my Brother also will with all heartiness accompany me.

I am sorry to hear of Mrs C.'s indisposition, but trust it will be only temporary. I was not aware that night, till I left you, how it stood with the poor youth, and that he stood on the eve of man's first calamity, exile from his Father's hearth. I wish I had shaken hands with him, and bidden him audibly Good Speed.

My scriptory ware still lies in the scales, which way inclining I cannot say, except in the spirit of a Prophet that ever prophecyeth _evil._ On Saturday I shall perhaps know more. Meanwhile, as ever, it is our part to defy the Devil, whether he come in the shape of Bookseller or another. I stay to say always: A fig for thee Nicholas!

Your Letter to Wilkie I shall with my earliest convenience deliver. Many thanks for it!

Ever Yours,

T. Carlyle.

)

Sunny Bank
1856 (Aug?)
August 12
Haddington

My dear Mr Tait

I do think you are
the kindest man alive! Thank
you with all my heart for the
beautiful little photographs —
If you only knew how they
are valued here!
Your letter was forwarded
from Auchtertool to this place.
My little Birthplace, god bless
it! — I came to stay three
days, but the three days had
to turn to ten — The dear
old ladies I am staying
with cried so when I spoke
of going yesterday. Oh how

I should like to show you these
old Ladies! the one eighty
the other eightysix — and they
are as clear minded and
warm hearted as ever they
were in their lives — and
look so pretty! like the
good Fairies they used to
tell me about when I sat
on their knees a pretty while
ago! — and their house reminds
me of the "beautiful house
among trees" that the "good
boy" who "sent to poos his
fortune (in their Tales) arrived
at always — and where

in all comfort and stillness,
he found "every thing on earth
that he needed" — Oh Mr
Tait, these dear old women
are a rehabilitation of old age
for one after the horrid
guys in London — after
having been familiarized with
that disreputable old age
that dies its hair and
bares its neck and arms
and seeks "distraction" at
Parties!

Do you know I think
dear old Scotland so much
better in every respect than
"the South" that I should

like to come back to it for
altogether - and have you
and two or three more London
people come to stay with
me in the summer -

What on earth does one get
by living amidst all that
dirt and dearth and din
but sick nerves and wearing
and vexation of spirit!

I was grown as cold and
hard as a stone, with continual
pressure of ill health and worry
- now I am so soft that I
fall a-crying twenty times a day
with sheer gratitude to everybody for
making so much of me &!

a miniature of Mrs. Carlyle's mother, who died fourteen years before the date of this letter.] Your letter was forwarded from Auchtertool to this place, my little birthplace God bless it!—I came to stay three days but the three days had to turn to ten.— The dear old ladies I am staying with cried so when I spoke of going yesterday. Oh how I should like to show you these old ladies! the one eighty the other eighty six, and they are as clear minded and warm hearted as ever they were in their lives, and look so pretty! like the Good Fairies they used to tell me about when I sat on their knees a pretty while ago!—And their house reminds me of the "beautiful house among trees" that the "good boy" who "went to poos his fortune" (in their Tales) arrived at always—and where in all comfort and stillness he found "everything on earth that he needed." Oh Mr. Tait! these dear old women are a rehabilitation of old age for one after the horrid guys in London!—after having been familiarized with that disreputable old age that dies its hair and bares its neck and arms and seeks "distraction" at parties!

Do you know I think dear old Scotland so much better in every respect than "the South" that I should like to come back to it for altogether—and have you and two or three more London people come to stay with me in the summer.

What on earth does one get by living amidst all that dirt and dearth and din but sick nerves and weariness and vexation of spirit?

I was grown as cold and hard as a stone, with continued pressure of ill health and worry.—Now I am so soft that I fall a-crying twenty times a day with sheer gratitude to everybody for making so much of me!

. . . . Yours affec⁣ᵗ,
JANE W. CARLYLE.

Delightful "feelings." Yet it was Mrs. Carlyle, quite as much as her husband, who, when the pinch of actual decision came, shrank from seconding the proposed "retreat to the desert." The old age that " dies " its hair is a quaint slip.

The other is a gay little note written from the house at Willesden of Mr. Neuberg, her husband's old friend and travelling companion.

To Mr. Robert Tait.

Saturday [5th July, 1856].

No Mr. Tait! I am not in Scotland—nor on the road to Scotland! I am sitting at this moment on one of Mr. Neuberg's thick-stuffed chairs at Willesden !!! In two hours I shall be please God in my own house, at Chelsea if it have not be[en] burnt down over night. And to morrow (Sunday) if you choose to come and see me you may!

The meaning of all this will be something to tell when you come. I slept here last night! That is to say I might have slept; if Nero had not behaved in a way that I shall not soon forget.

Bexhill—Yes I suppose I shall go to Bexhill on Monday—I don't know for certain—I don't know anything for certain except that Nero is head and ears in love with "Mrs. Tott-oonter's" spaniel. What an absurd creature a dog in love is! almost as absurd as a man!

Yours sincerely,

Jane W. Carlyle.

. "Nero," it will be remembered, was the little spaniel to which Mrs. Carlyle was greatly devoted, and which was painted by Mr. Tait in his picture of the Cheyne Row dining-room. Her affection for this little companion was intense, and when "Nero" came to an untimely end, four years later, his mistress wrote a

quaintly pathetic letter to her artist friend, begging for two
small photographs of the picture, that her faithful four-legged
comrade might be embodied in brooches for herself and the
maid, who was going red-eyed and tearful about her house-work!
The drawings from the

Cast of Carlyle's Head

(in the possession of my father) are interesting phrenologically,
and as giving the outline of the brow and head; but the plaster
replica is as disappointing and unsatisfactory in other respects
as these masks generally are. The operation is always a delicate
and difficult one, and in this instance Sir Edgar Boehm and his
assistant had a specially arduous task. Beyond the changes and
muscular relaxation which follow death, the recumbent position,
and the flattening of beard and hair, of course, further affect the
appearance. In the present case the form of the nose seemed
to me so different from the life as to make me doubt the correct-
ness of the impression; but I have since seen two careful pencil
drawings which Mrs. Allingham was permitted to make after
death, in which precisely the same alteration of feature is indicated, and which generally confirm the accuracy of the cast.
On the small

Plans

of the various floors at 5, Cheyne Row, I have indicated, as far
as was possible, the arrangement of the rooms, and have added
some descriptive notes in the text; but, of course, the periodic
"earthquakes" resulted in shiftings and changes which hardly
called for detailed chronicle here.

Carlyle's Seal,

the drawing from an impression of which is given at the end of
the book, was cut from a sketch made by himself in 1823. The

emblem is the wasting candle, and the motto, "May I be wasted so that I be of use." "But what if I do not *prosum*?" he wrote, beneath it; "why then *terar* still, so I cannot help it. This is the end and the beginning of all philosophy; we must just do the best we can. Oh, most lame and impotent conclusion."

The Head and Tail-pieces

throughout the book are, it need hardly be said, quotations from Carlyle's works.

DRAWING FROM IMPRESSION OF A SEAL CUT FROM SKETCH
MADE BY CARLYLE.

A sore fight: but
he won it.

INDEX.

INDEX.

CHISWICK PRESS:—CHARLES WHITTINGHAM AND CO.,
TOOKS COURT, CHANCERY LANE, LONDON.

A CENTENARY MEMORIAL,
1895.

Thoughts on Life

BY

THOMAS CARLYLE.

SELECTED BY ROBERT DUNCAN.

This volume contains a PORTRAIT IN PHOTOGRAVURE,
and is published by MESSRS. CHAPMAN AND
HALL, LIMITED, *in three forms, viz. :*

In PAPER COVERS, at One Shilling.

In CLOTH BINDING, at Eighteenpence.

In LEATHER BINDING, on handmade Paper, and with
· Portrait on Japanese Paper, at Five Shillings.

*The Editor's share of the Proceeds will be devoted
to the* CENTENARY MEMORIAL FUND.